Compiled and edited by Roger Fawcett-Tang
Essays by William Owen

Mapping graphic navigational systems

02 Inhabitable space

00_Introduction

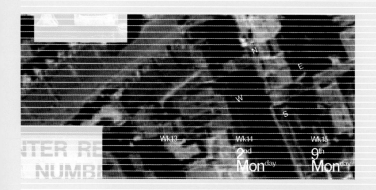

Beyond the horizon

Essay by William Owen
010/011

What is a map?
Maps inhabit the realm of fact, although not exclusively. They are figurative representations of dimensions, attributes and relations of things in the physical or logical world, reproduced at a scale smaller than life-size (usually, but not exclusively – sometimes their scale is 1:1 or, when mapping the microcosm, larger).

What can be mapped?
Anything can be mapped, and most things are: places, businesses, galaxies, histories, bodies, philosophies, devices and databases. The subject-matter of a map is measured, named and ordered (captured!) by the mapmaker who, armed with carefully verified data and a language of pictorial description, puts everything in its proper place with its proper name as he or she sees it.

Why make maps?
Maps give their makers the power to define the territory in their terms and write a singular vision onto the landscape. Princes, popes and governments have used maps to exert their rights, extend their trade, tax their subjects and know their enemies. Oil magnates use maps to locate and claim the earth. Newspapers use maps to tell stories of war and peace. Social scientists use maps to publicise social problems. A city resident sketches a map to bring a friend from the station by the shortest or most interesting route – the mapmaker decides.

Anything can be mapped, and most things are: places, businesses, galaxies, histories, bodies, philosophies, devices and databases.

Why use maps?

Maps give their readers the simple and magical ability to see beyond the horizon. The enlightening and revelatory characteristic of a good map derives from its encompassing vision, contained within a single consistent pictorial model. The map provides a view that slides instantaneously between panorama and detail. A map embodies the work, knowledge and intelligence of others. We obtain a vision of a place that we may never have seen, or divine a previously unseen pattern in things we thought we knew intimately. So, we 'consult' a map as we would an adviser in order to locate, identify and decide, or to be enlightened. As a result we suffer, sometimes, a grand illusion of omnipotence by believing that the map contains everything necessary for understanding or controlling a domain. We forget that the mapmaker has an implicit or explicit agenda of his own, not necessarily aligned with ours. Maps are imperfect. They have missing layers and gaps within the layers ("London", said its 'biographer' Peter Ackroyd, "is so large, and so diverse, that a thousand different maps or topographies have been drawn up in order to describe it"). Paradoxically, much information can be gathered from the gaps left in maps, not least about the mapmaker's intentions. This is one of the beauties of maps.

Are maps true?

Maps are man-made things and so are neither arbitrary nor pure. They purport to be 'natural' and objective visual representations arising out of scientific observation, and yet the observations are selective and they must be translated and communicated through some graphic form: the scientist (or surveyor) relies on the cartographer's art to illustrate his findings.

What gives maps their power?

Maps are seen by their readers as neutral carriers of information, and thus have the power to persuade without appearing to do so "because the myths they contain are naturalised within a system of 'facts'".[1]

This naturalness inhabits the language and conventions of maps, which comprises a value-laden semiological system. Maps contain clear hierarchies that influence how we see the world. For example, Ptolemy chose to orient north at the top of the map, and mapmakers have followed his precedent ever since. There is no good reason for this other than convention, but the effect is to create a hierarchy of the earth and the idea that a particular view is 'correct'. This is just one of a system of signs and therefore of values that constitute cartography. The language of cartography is so ingrained that it has become invisible. We do not question the connection between the blue line on the map and the idea of a 'river', or that roads should be anything other than two black parallel lines (of a width apart that almost never conforms to the actual scale of the map). We see the signifier and signified as equivalents, one deriving naturally out of the other. It is quite natural to us that north should always be at the top, a round world transformed into a flat plane, a particular thematic selection made, a certain scale chosen. The cartographer, therefore, has a heavy responsibility to be frank about his choices and their effect on the use and value of the map.

The language of cartography is so ingrained that it has become invisible. We do not question the connection between the blue line on the map and the idea of a 'river', or that roads should be anything other than two black parallel lines.

[1] Denis Wood,
'The Power of Maps',
The Guilford Press,
New York, 1992.

Beyond the horizon

Nick Bell Design
Lost and
Found exhibit
130/131

Essay by William Owen
012/013

How do maps work?

Cartography has an arsenal of iconographic, geometric, linguistic and formal conventions with which to mediate source data into pictorial representation. Maps require geometric translations (of a 3D world onto a 2D plane) or transformations (scaling from 1:1 to 1: n), editorial selections (what is shown, what is ignored), and iconographic representation.

Two systems of signs are used predominantly to define attributes and dimensions: firstly icons, which normally define a general attribute or dimensional range (what order of object is this? a city, of between 50-100,000 inhabitants); and secondly text, to describe specific attributes (what name, who are the owners, how old is it, how big?).

There are four further sign systems – metapatterns that occur repeatedly in maps and which define spatial relations and dimensions: the matrix (also known as the chloropleth), which marks boundaries and divisions, where one area becomes another and what lies next to what; the network, which shows systems of flow, such as drainage, communication, navigation; the point, which marks the position of discrete objects within a space, such as settlements, landmarks or buildings; the nested layer, which reveals continuums of equality, as in contour lines marking equal height or isobars marking equal air pressure. Each of these sign systems exists within the context of a fifth, the axes or coordinates of the map, which frame the absolute relations of one point to another and define the limit of the map (and in extremes the edge of the known world).

How far can we stretch the meaning of 'map'?

The metapatterns – matrix, network, point and nest – are adaptable to an infinite range of non-geographic narratives. Activities that have a relation to physical space, such as social or commercial systems, usually adopt a geographical metaphor and are clearly accepted as maps by Western convention, Mechanical, electronic or biological systems, such as the human body or electronic circuits, can be represented topologically or topographically. Mapping can be applied to ideas and information, to logical[1] systems of philosophy, religion, science and taxonomy, and even to allegorical or fictional accounts of social and political relations – Jonathan Swift's map of Gulliver's Travels is surely no less 'real' than Ortelius' atlas of the world, although one is merely mimicking the scientific language of the other. We tend, in Western culture, to restrict our definition of maps to faithfully scaled reproductions of linear spatial relations. Islamic and South Indian art pushes metapatterns much further, to create intuitive topological representations of human or physical relations independent of spatial dimensions. Such constructs are, potentially, a richly-layered, non-linear, multi-perspective communication model for the networked digital society, and they are no less maps.

[1] Logic in the Hegelian sense, as the fundamental science of thought and its categories including metaphysics or ontology.

Cartography has an arsenal of iconographic, geometric, linguistic and formal conventions with which to mediate source data into pictorial representation.

Lust
Kern DH map
138/139

Nina Naegal
and A. Kanna
Time/Emotions
198/199

Where and when are maps?

Maps and fragments of maps are everywhere at any time. Maps now have no beginning or end, merging with networked devices within other traditionally discrete objects: the map, the key, the guidebook, the wallet, the phone, the camera – all one thing. In-car navigation systems speak your route. Global positioning systems plot your coordinates and altitude. Head-up displays throw the map onto your personal vision of the landscape. Third generation mobile phones know who you are, where you are, what's near you, who is near you, even what you want. The phone becomes the map. Digital maps have multiple scales for zooming to capture details, with multiple digital layers for different themes. You choose: transport? drainage? buildings? heritage? Geographical Information Systems define millions of objects as discrete data points each with their own logical address, to which any amount of data can be attached, and so the map merges with the database table and the table is interrogated through the map. Changing the database changes the map so that at last the map keeps pace with the landscape, released from the inertia and inefficiencies of print. The future of maps is to vanish into all of these things, and reappear in everything.

Maps now have no beginning or end, merging within networked devices within other traditionally discrete objects: the map, the key, the guidebook, the wallet, the phone, the camera - all one thing.

01_Representation and space

You are here...

Essay by William Owen
016/017

Inuit hunters carve three-dimensional charts of the coastlines around Greenland and Eastern Canada out of driftwood (and have done for over 300 years). These maps are highly functional and abstracted. The critical datum line provided by the land-sea boundary is represented by the flat edge of the carved wood – the chart is meant to be fingered on a dark night in a kayak out at sea – but the topography of islands and the features around coastal inlets are clearly represented in three dimensions in the curve and bulk of the wood. These maps fit easily in the hand and they are weatherproof and fumbleproof (if they are dropped overboard, they float). They also have no up or down, so orientation or hierarchy is not an issue, and neither are the problems of transformation from the real three-dimensional world to the flat land of maps[1]. These carved pieces are masterpieces of design.

Light-aircraft pilots – not a world away from the Inuit in their navigational preoccupations – use two-dimensional aviation charts that represent a bewilderingly complex three-dimensional land, sea and airscape. The design of these charts is in vivid contrast with the Inuit driftwood objects. Like most Western maps, aviation charts are, of course, printed on paper, with three dimensions flattened into two by projection. Linear thematic layers are stratified one atop another and read (not fingered, smelled or tasted) by the eye and the mind of a rational observer who is familiar with a myriad of signs. The family of signs – symbols, icons and indices – that comprise the language of maps, here signifies the perilous reality of civil aviation routes, airport exclusion zones, military airspace, microwave towers, radio navigation beacons and high ground on the landscape.

The aviation chart is an extreme example of the tortuous transformation from three dimensions to two because, in addition to the ground features that provide relational information, there are many different kinds of volumes of airspace to be negotiated, each with their own permissions, rules and other characteristics. The pilot flies through these or around them: not just over them, but also above, under and between them. In a busy and feature-laden airspace like that around southern England, the problem of spatial orientation and interpretation is acute; a highly refined sign-reading is critical to survival or the retention of one's flying licence. How a pilot must, sometimes, envy the intuitive instrument available to his kayaking counterpart.

The degree to which this chart is abstracted out of the reality of physical land, air and water is astounding – although in part this is merely because the abstraction is so evident. Many of the features indicated on the aviation chart, for example, have no physical reality. An airport exclusion zone is a man-made abstraction designed to control movement where there are no natural physical points of orientation (no traffic lights or curbstones in the sky!) although its existence is no less real in the pilot's mind. The zone is represented on the map by a combination of icons (signing airport and its position), index (boundary lines and coloured hatching indicating the extent and type of the exclusion zone) and symbols (text showing the name and altitude of the zone). This signification of abstract and physical entities applies to all maps to a greater or lesser degree and we have assimilated the language thoroughly into our consciousness. Having seen the name of a city represented on a map at scale, would we expect to see the same name printed in mile-wide text across the ground of the real world? Of course not, but why not? The language of maps that we have grown up with and that seems so natural and realistic has, nonetheless, a coded grammar and vocabulary that would be quite meaningless to an Inuit kayaker of 300 years ago.

The mediation that takes place during the transformation from the most objective survey data to readable map occurs at numerous levels and its result is an entirely subjective narrative.

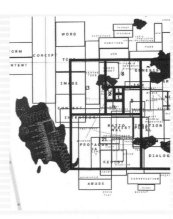

The mediation that takes place during the transformation from the most objective scientific survey data to readable map occurs at numerous levels and its result is an entirely subjective narrative. The most fundamental of these and the least visible are projection, orientation and scale. Projection gives a point of view, orientation creates a hierarchy, and scale provides an understanding of time and horizon – how far do we need to see and how far are we going. We don't need to be told that a 1:25,000 map is for walkers – anyone travelling faster needs a wider focus and less detail. It is telling that most single sheet maps contain within one view the distance a person can travel in half a day. 1:25,000 is 20-30 km across, being three to four hours walking at 6kph; 1:50,000 is 40-60 km across, being three hours cycling at 20kph; 1:300,000 is 150 km across, being three hours motoring at 50kph. A glance at the scale tells us the audience and purpose for the map.

The narrative is told by numerous factors that are extrinsic to the map itself. These are things that are not in the picture plane but inform it and establish context: the legend establishes a rhetorical style ('Classical Rome', 'Water: precious resource', 'pathfinder', 'streetwise'); unspoken but implicit themes are revealed by gaps in the mapped layers. (Think of the map of a seaside town that shows beaches but not sewage outfalls – the narrative is one of unsullied leisure without duty of care or acknowledging unpleasant reality.) There is also the utility of the map – why was it made and by whom, which might be revealed by some historical legacy such as the name Ordnance Survey (this map first served a military purpose) or the residue from a bygone age of travelling in the special signs for rural inns and public houses but none for contemporary urban coffee bars.

Other signs are intrinsic to the map itself – its icons and their correspondence to the objects they represent; its language, and how it elaborates on other signs; its tectonic codes and how they shape the space through projection, scale or indices; its temporal codes which are critical to the narrative form (most maps include only those classes of objects which are expected to remain static for a certain period of time – which could be a minute but is more likely to be a decade); its overall presentation, the style and tone of the imagery, which may be soft or loud, high or low contrast, luxurious or functional, whimsical or idealistic.

An example of the use of style and symbolic presentation in the subtle service of rhetoric is the GeoSphere project cited by Denis Wood[2]. Described by its publishers, National Geographic, as a 'global portrait' (i.e. photograph) this was a popular image of the earth created from satellite data by artist Tom Van Sant. The map presents itself as a photograph, a true image of the earth. It is nonetheless a map, comprised of indexical signs and therefore no more 'real' or 'natural' than any other map. In his deconstruction of the image, Wood notes that the 'Portrait' is first of all a flat picture of a round planet, with the world stretched and distorted to fit into a rectangle using the Robinson projection. The image is reproduced at scale, and its resolution is no greater than one pixel per square kilometre. The image caters to our perceptions of 'naturalness', its colours are false; there are no clouds visible whatsoever (the image is captioned 'a clear day' – one miraculously so), and – this is the clincher – there is no night: the entire surface of the globe is bathed in sunlight, and this last point is the least obvious to the casual observer when one asks what exactly is 'wrong' with this image.

[1] Victor Papanek,
'The Green Imperative:
natural design for the real
world.' Thames and Hudson,
1995 (cited by George H. Brett,
www.deadmedia.org)

[2] 'The Power of Maps', ibid

Design	Willi Kunz Associates
Project	Programme information posters
Client	Columbia University

Columbia University
Graduate School of Architecture
Planning and Preservation

Master
of Science
in

and

Architecture | Urban Design

Program
Emphasis
Emphasis
Resources

The Master of Science Degree in Architecture and Urban Design has been reformulated beginning in 1992-1993. It is an intensive three semester program for architects interested in post-professional specialization.

The curriculum is oriented toward the emerging urbanism in the United States, with a particular emphasis on the situation in New York City. It seeks to define parameters and problems which will carry into the next century. It also embraces a special relationship between the design studio and New York, through collaboration with city agencies and other public interest constituencies. Comparative study with other world cities is also considered central to the pedagogic structure, focused on seminars and case studies.

The degree is intended to augment traditional professional training in architecture for those who wish to further investigate the physical aspects of urbanism. 'Urban Design' is seen as an activist, social art, more than a singular representation of physical scale; the term defines a commitment to discourse at all scales of design activity. In this sense, the unique situation of Columbia allows New York City to become a laboratory, in which the discipline of architecture can be applied to a myriad of problems within our urban enviroment at all scales of inquiry. At the same time, the more theoretical component of coursework allows for comparative study with other world cities and situations. The design studio is the primary catalyst for the curriculum, centered on a highly individualized, atelier approach.

The Columbia University Graduate School of Architecture, Planning and Preservation is a unique academic forum within which to pursue studies in Urban Design. The distinguished, multidisciplinary faculty nurtures a wideranging critical perspective on the question of urbanism today. Classroom and studio teaching is reinforced by extensive lecture and publication programs. The Avery Architectural and Fine Arts Library is an invaluable resource, as the nation's finest repository for the literature of architecture, planning, and fine arts. In addition, the innumerable cultural resources of New York City, as a whole, are close at hand.

Bernard Tschumi, Dean

Richard Plunz, Director

Further information and application
Columbia University
Office of Architecture Admissions
400 Avery Hall
New York, NY 10027
212 854 3414

Two posters produced for Columbia University. The first poster announces a programme in architecture and urban design at the university. It incorporates a series of black and white images arranged in a stepped formation to suggest the gradual expansion from city to industrial environment. The strong grid lines in the aerial photography have a close relation to the cityscape photograph in the bottom left corner, helping to form a fluid link through the various images. The staggered layout of images is echoed in the thick irregular frame that contains the poster.

The second poster was designed to announce an undergraduate programme in architecture, urban planning, and historic preservation held in New York and Paris. The poster shows simplified maps of the two cities, placing the map of New York's Manhattan within a square which echoes the nature of the street plan, and placing Paris within a circle, again illustrating the more organic nature of that city's street plan. The overlapping of the two maps helps to create a dynamic tension between the two cities.

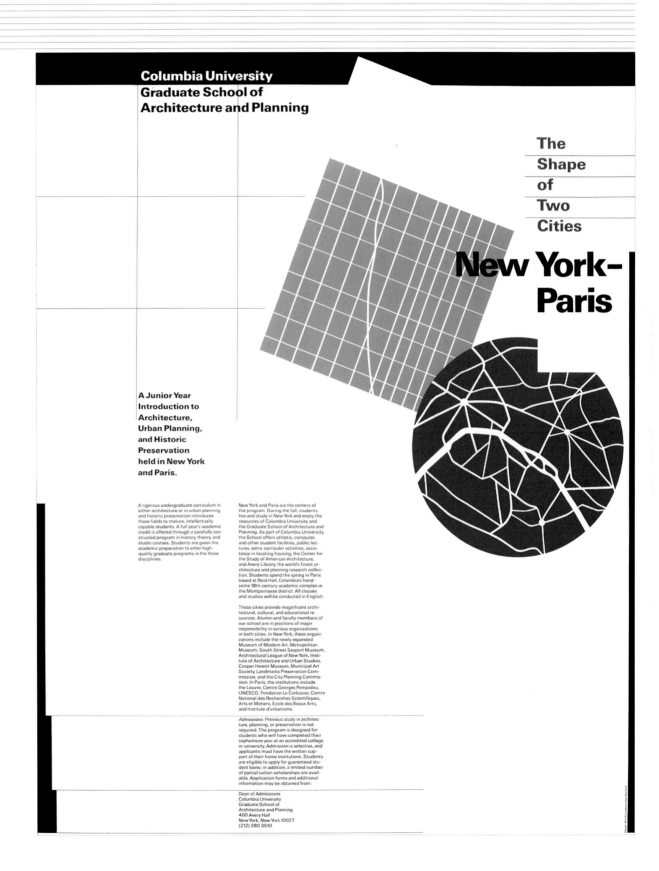

Design   Imagination
Project   The Journey zone

The Journey zone was the exhibition dealing with the subject of transportation at the UK's Millennium Dome, a network of exhibition pavilions designed to mark the new millennium. As the work of the multi-disciplinary design company Imagination, the building's architecture and the exhibition graphic were considered together, and the graphic design works to lead visitors around the exhibition, to create coherence throughout the building and to describe the nature of transportation and movement.

In the sample shown here, each panel graphically represents a different mode of travel/transport. By using and adapting the existing graphic language for each one, the viewer, with a little vision, can recognise the mode of transport being illustrated: motorways, flight paths, rail routes, footpaths and bridleways, and so on. Individually these graphic elements do not convey any precise information – they are purely stylistic illustrations derived from the language of mapping which, if nothing else, illustrate to the viewer the myriad ways that movement can be expressed using simple lines and arrows – but together they provide an innovative form of signage leading the visitor around a complex walk-though exhibition.

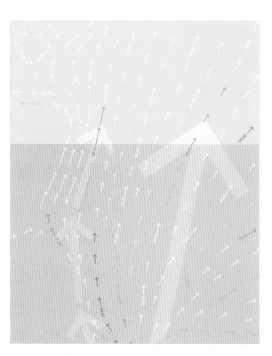

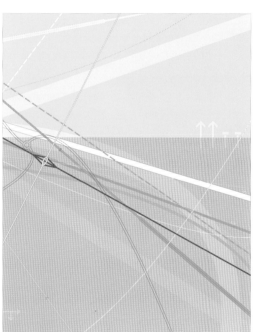

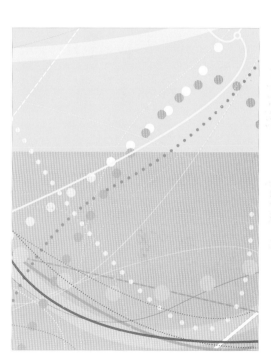

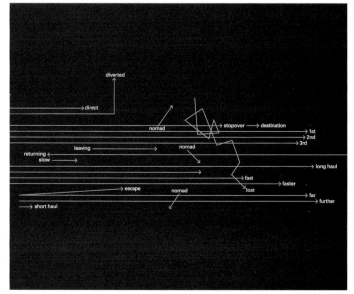

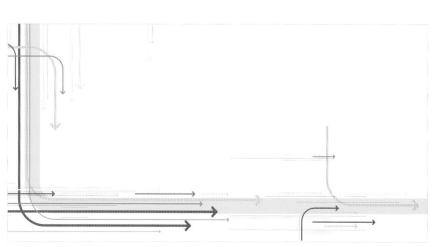

Design   Struktur Design
Project   Ideas 2007 Conference

Ideas2007: Creativity Beyond Borders
The First Middle East and North Africa Creativity Congress

www.cbb2007.com

creativity
beyond
borders

A series of vector-based physical maps were used for the identity and promotional material for the Ideas 2007 creativity conference held in Dubai and Abu Dhabi, UAE. The maps, which focus on the Middle East, were edited from the convetional colour palette associated with mapping, and became increasingly abstracted with each poster or leaflet. Various layers of the vector-based maps were removed, and certain levels of the relief maps add a further degree of abstraction - from the ocean floor to the highest mountain range.

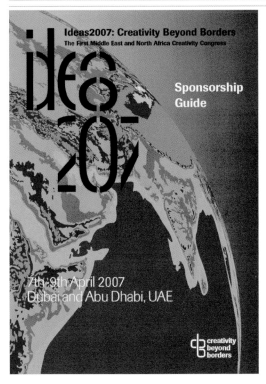

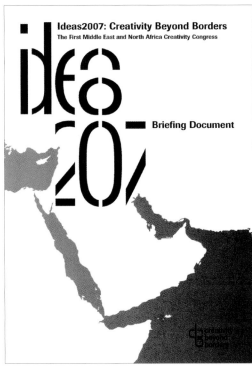

Design   Cartlidge Levene
Project   Pattern poster for Blanka's 'Mono' exhibition

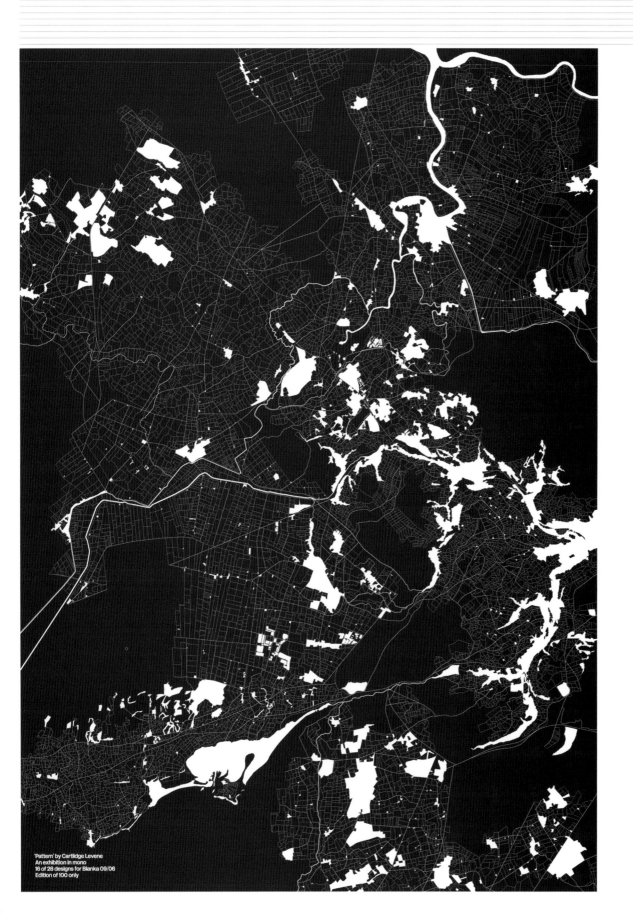

'Pattern' by Cartlidge Levene
An exhibition in mono
16 of 28 designs for Blanka 09/06
Edition of 100 only

28 leading European graphic design studios were invited
by Blanka to design a poster for their 'Mono' exhibition.
Each designer was asked to produce an A1 (23⅖ x 33¹⁄₁₀in)
black and white poster based on a given design related
word. Cartlidge Levene's word was 'pattern'. Their
inspiration came from working on various urban mapping
projects. The poster explores the patterns and textures
created by fields, hedges, walls, rivers and woods that,
when converted to a negative, appear abstract.

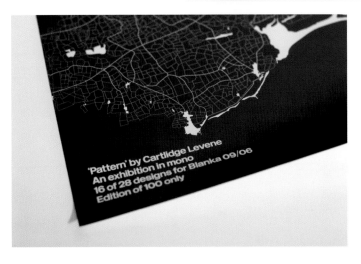

Artist	Simon Patterson	Artist	Simon Patterson
Title	'J.P.233 in C.S.O. Blue'	Title	'The Great Bear'
Dimensions	Variable	Dimensions	43 x 53in (1092 x 1346mm)
Photography	Matthias Hermann	Copyright	Simon Patterson and London Regional Transport
Image courtesy	The Lisson Gallery, London	Photography	John Riddy
		Image courtesy	The Lisson Gallery, London

The artist Simon Patterson, a finalist for the Turner Prize, the UK's leading award for modern art, has worked extensively with the process of reinterpreting existing information systems. Shown here are two works by the artist which utilise maps and navigation/information systems.

'J.P.233 in C.S.O. Blue' is a large wall drawing which takes as its reference a global airline route map, using large sweeping arcs to represent the journeys between countries, which are implied by their relative positions rather than a delineation of boundaries. The destination names are replaced with seemingly unrelated famous people, from Julius Caesar, Elizabeth I, Pope John-Paul II and Mussolini to actors William Shatner, Helen Mirren, Leonard Nimoy and Peter Falk.

In 'The Great Bear', Patterson begins with a very famous reference point, the map of the London Underground, possibly the best-known and most copied subway map, which was itself first developed by Henry Beck in the 1930s. The London Underground map is most notable for the way it distorts and simplifies the physical spaces it represents, in order to provide the most effective presentation of the relationships between lines and stations, and aid the viewer with planning journeys on which there are few visible landmarks. In 'The Great Bear', Patterson remains faithful to the original London Underground map, but replaces all station names with a variety of famous names. Each line on the network plays host to a particular category of famous people - the Circle line stations take on the names of philosophers, for example, while the Northern line becomes a list of film actors. This replacement of names disorients the viewer: at first glance the map looks familiar – until, that is, one tries to find a particular tube stop, then it becomes increasingly difficult, because all the points of reference have been changed.

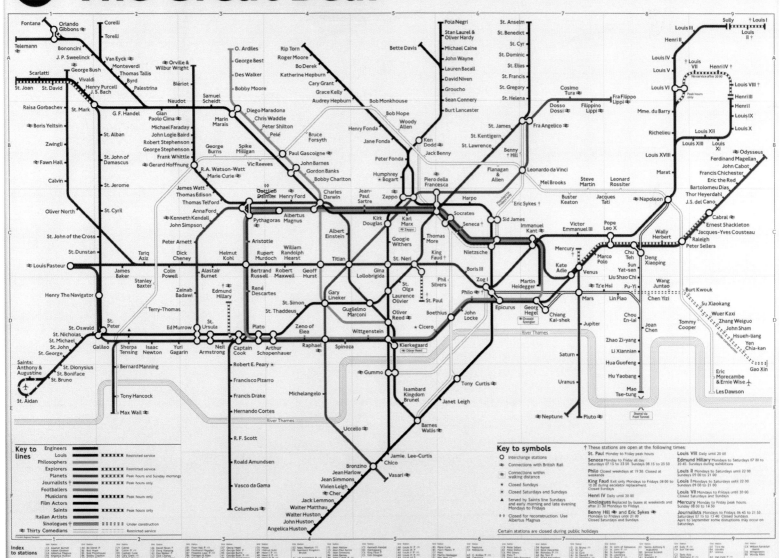

Artist	Simon Patterson
Title	'Untitled: 24 hrs'
Image courtesy	The Lisson Gallery, London

Artist	Simon Patterson
Title	'Rhodes Reason'
Image courtesy	The Lisson Gallery, London

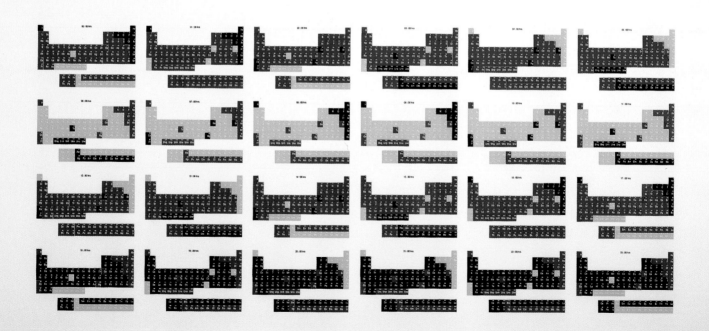

Two further works by the artist Simon Patterson both refer to the Periodic Table, pinned up on the wall of every school chemistry lab. This typographic work of beauty is frequently plagiarised by other graphic designers, but here it is taken to a higher level. 'Untitled: 24hrs' reproduces the table 24 times. Each table is printed in four colours; the first row of tables are predominantly blue, the second row yellow, then red and finally black. The colours refer to a property of each substance: Black = Solid, Red = Gas, Blue = Liquid and Yellow = Synthetically Prepared. The same colour palette is also used in 'Rhodes Reason', which again features the odd film star, for example Kim Novak (Na 11) is Sodium, while Telly Savalas (As 33) is Arsenic. Rhodes Reason was also published as a book called Rex Reason.

Rhodes Reason

Key:

Group Classifications [1]	
Atomic Number	26
Symbol [2]	Fe
Name	Fred MacMurray

Period	1 (IA)	2 (IIA)	3 (IIIA)	4 (IVA)	5 (VA)	6 (VIA)	7 (VIIA)	8/9/10 (VIII)			11 (IB)	12 (IIB)	13 (IIIB)	14 (IVB)	15 (VB)	16 (VIB)	17 (VIIB)	18 (VIII/0)
1	1 H Hyperion																	2 He Helios
2	3 Li Bela Lugosi	4 Be Ingrid Bergman											5 B Ingmar Bergman	6 C Capucine	7 N Niobe	8 O Orpheus	9 F Flora	10 Ne Nereus
3	11 Na Kim Novak	12 Mg Patrick McGoohan											13 Al Alec McCowen	14 Si Simone Signoret	15 P Patrick MacNee	16 S Steve McQueen	17 Cl Cybele	18 Ar Ariadne
4	19 K Grace Kelly	20 Ca Claudia Cardinale	21 Sc Sean Connery	22 Ti Yoko Tani	23 V Josef Von Sternberg	24 Cr Conrad Veidt	25 Mn F.W. Murnau	26 Fe Fred MacMurray	27 Co Federico Fellini	28 Ni Tatsuya Nakadai	29 Cu Tony Curtis	30 Zn Fred Zinnemann	31 Ga Ghirlandaio	32 Ge George Eastman	33 As Telly Savalas	34 Se Peter Sellers	35 Br Bronzino	36 Kr Kronos
5	37 Rb Red Buttons	38 Sr Erich Von Stroheim	39 Y Loretta Young	40 Zr Adolph Zukor	41 Nb Nigel Bruce	42 Mo Yves Montand	43 Tc Technetium	44 Ru Jane Russell	45 Rh Rex Harrison	46 Pd Walter Pidgeon	47 Ag Alec Guinness	48 Cd Candice Bergen	49 In Rex Ingram	50 Sn Susan Sarandon	51 Sb Sarah Bernhardt	52 Te Tex Ritter	53 I Ken Ichikawa	54 Xe Xantippe
6	55 Cs Cesare da Sesto	56 Ba Bibi Andersson	57 La Lana Turner	72 Hf Henry Fonda	73 Ta Elizabeth Taylor	74 W Billy Wilder	75 Re Rex Reason	76 Os Rhodes Reason	77 Ir Ub Iwerks	78 Pt Rip Torn	79 Au Audrey Hepburn	80 Hg Hugo van der Goes	81 Tl Robert Taylor	82 Pb Peter Bogdanovich	83 Bi Juliette Binoche	84 Po Roman Polanski	85 At Andrei Tarkovsky	86 Rn Rhianus
7	87 Fr Fra Filippo Lippi	88 Ra Vivienne Romance	89 Ac Anjelica Huston	104 Unq Unnilquadium	105 Unp Unnilpentium	106 Unh Unnilhexium	107 Uns Unnilseptium	108 Uno Unniloctium	109 Une Unnilenium									

Lanthanide Series

58 Ce Lon Chaney	59 Pr Dita Parlo	60 Nd David Niven	61 Pm Promethium	62 Sm Spanky McFarland	63 Eu Edward Underdown	64 Gd Paulette Goddard	65 Tb Theda Bara	66 Dy Walt Disney	67 Ho John Huston	68 Er Emmanuelle Riva	69 Tm Toshiro Mifune	70 Yb Yul Brynner	71 Lu A & L Lumière

Actinide Series

90 Th Terry-Thomas	91 Pa Peggy Ashcroft	92 U Peter Ustinov	93 Np Neptunium	94 Pu Plutonium	95 Am Americium	96 Cm Curium	97 Bk Berkelium	98 Cf Californium	99 Es Einsteinium	100 Fm Fermium	101 Md Mendelevium	102 No Nobelium	103 Lr Lawrencium

1/ SMGP now recommends the numerical classification system given in the top row; however, some authorities prefer classification schemes that use A/B subgroup designations. Caution: A/B subgroup designations vary depending on the classification system used.

2/ Element symbol is colour-coded as follows:
Black = solid; Red = gas; Blue = liquid;
Yellow = synthetically prepared.

Simon Patterson 1995 30/60

Design   Cartlidge Levene
Project   Everything we have ever produced using Helvetica

Cartlidge Levene established 1987
Everything we have ever produced using Helvetica

As part of the '50 years of Helvetica' exhibition held at the Design Museum in London, Blanka and Candy Collective asked 50 designers to produce a 19¹¹/₁₆in (500mm) square poster. Cartlidge Levene's response was to chronologically map out every piece of their design output since the company was founded in 1987. Each sample is proportionally sized, creating an interesting mix of scale, from the smallest leaflet to the largest poster.

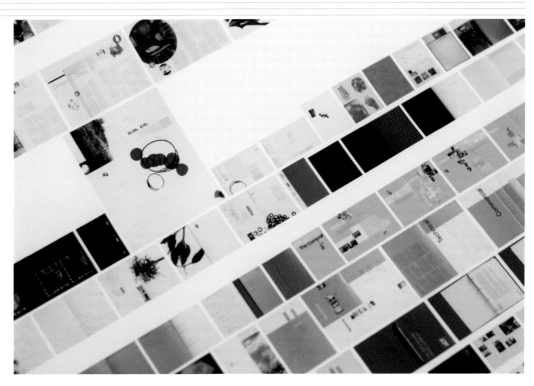

Design   Joost Grootens
Project   Limes Atlas

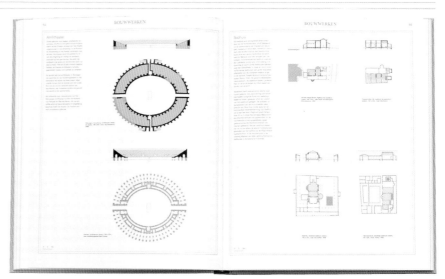

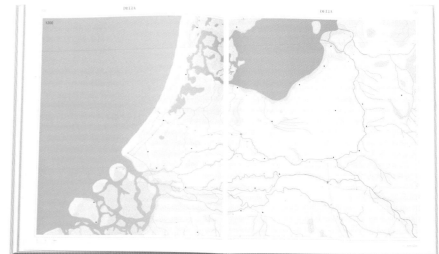

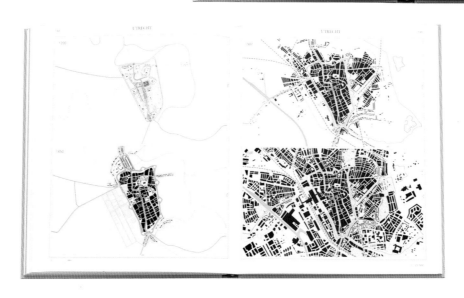

This atlas traces the northern boundary (limes) of the ancient Roman Empire, and follows its path through three Dutch cities: Nijmegen, Utrecht and Leiden. Referencing classical atlases, this book provides an in-depth study of how the Dutch landscape has been shaped since the Roman Empire by providing scale maps of the country and its cities and regions in the years 200, 1200, 1600, 1900 and 2000.

The atlas uses a carefully studied colour palette, including gold for all areas on the maps that represent real findings of the 'limes', as well as old Roman roads and fortresses. Custom patterns were designed for the maps.

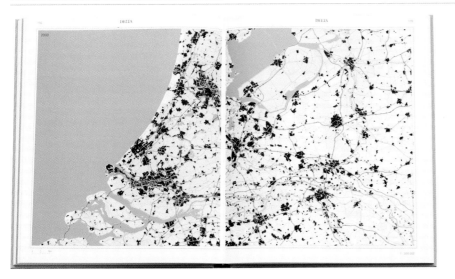

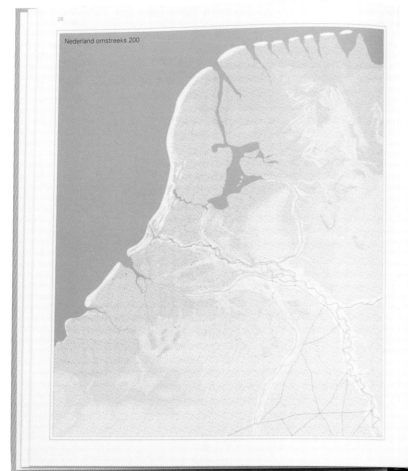

Design   NB: Studio
Project   London's Kerning

NB: Studio were approached by the International Society of Typographic Designers to create a piece of work for the 'My City, My London' exhibition, as part of the London Design Festival 2006. The exhibition celebrated the place of graphic design in contemporary visual culture, and its intention was to explore typography in the visual world of London. NB: Studio's solution was simple – to create a typographic map.

After removing graphic elements such as roads, rivers and parks from a map, all that remained was typography. The result is a map that, despite its sole use of typography, still clearly defines London's densely packed road system.

LONDON'S KERNING

Design   Pentagram
Project   'Sugar' interface for One Laptop Per Child

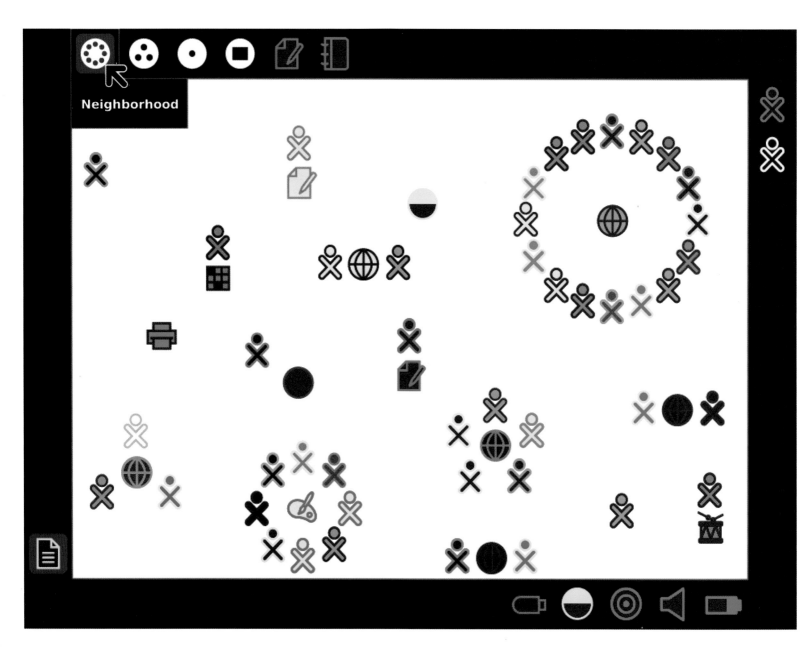

Pentagram created this laptop interface design for the One Laptop Per Child (OLPC) project, an initiative to provide children around the world with new opportunities to explore, experiment and express themselves. The designers worked in close collaboration with the OLPC development team. Rather than modeling the interface on a traditional computer desktop metaphor, 'Sugar' places the individual user at the centre of the icon-based interface, which has four levels of view: Home, Friends, Neighborhood and Activity. Users move outward from the Home view, where they can set preferences such as colour; to the Friends view, where they can chat with their friends; to the larger Neighborhood view, where they can locate other users and gather around an activity. The Activity view looks inward: children, alone or together, can focus on a particular project. In each view, a toolbar-like frame is available that organizes navigation, people and activities, and files around the four sides of view.

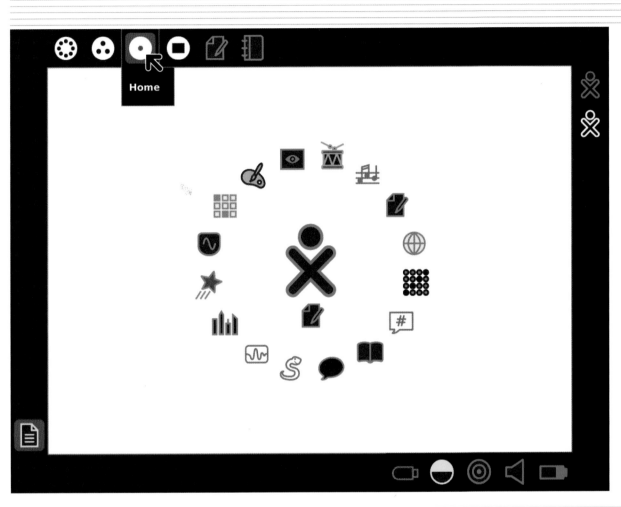

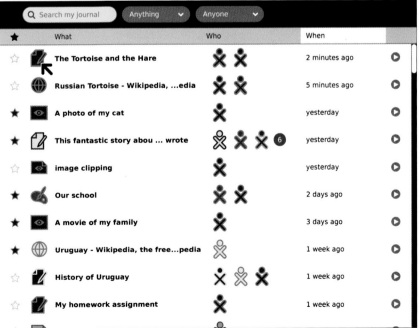

Design   The Kitchen
Project   Studio floorplan

This floorplan of the studio occupied by London-based design consultancy The Kitchen works as a graphic snapshot of the space at one moment in time. Each item within the space has been carefully itemised and catalogued, and the map visually represents their locations within the studio. While the shapes of the objects are abstracted, a complex coding system is used, where each item is assessed and allocated a unique colour which is derived from the colour used most prominently in the object. The positions of the objects are further referenced – or cross-referenced – through a list of co-ordinates. The map of the studio contains none of the features one might expect to find in an interior plan – no suggestion of walls, windows, doors and so on – but the physical shape, business and working patterns of the studio are revealed by the relative densities and positions of the objects found in different parts of the map.

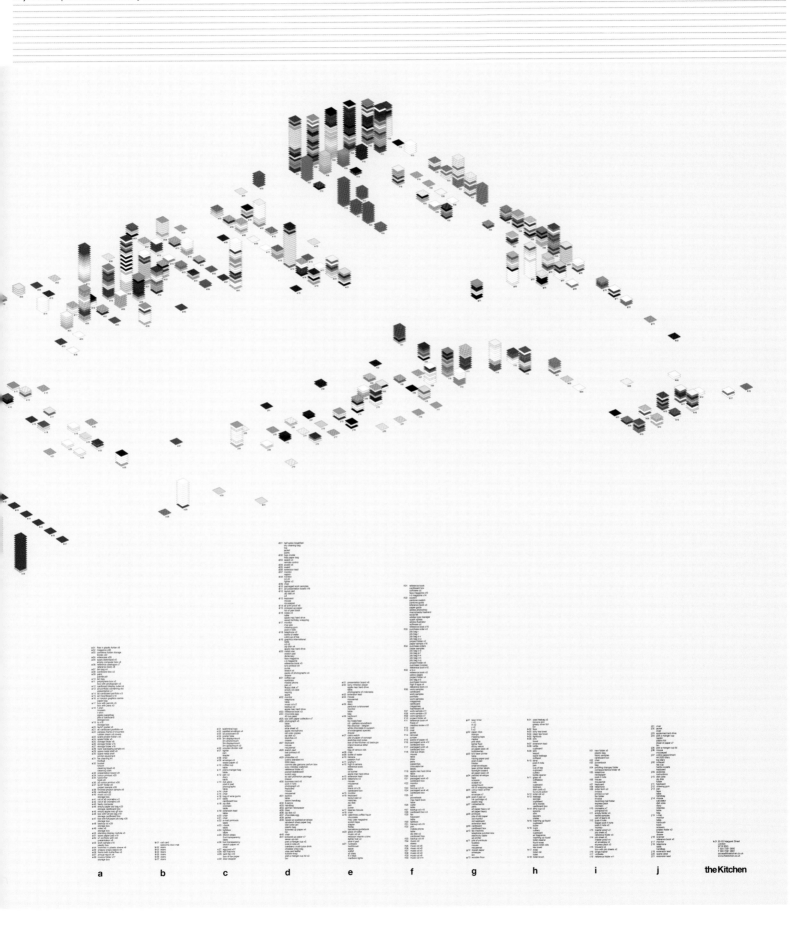

a b c d e f g h i j

the Kitchen

Design   Jeremy Johnson
Project   A visual record of the entire contents of a typecase

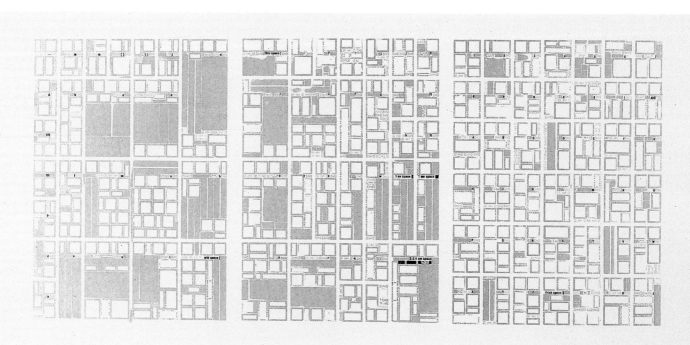

Produced as a visual record of the entire contents of a typecase at the Royal College of Art, London, over an 18-month period, this set of 12 16⁴⁷/₆₄ x 39³/₈in (425 x 1000mm) sheets was designed by Jeremy Johnson. The typographic inventories form clear maps showing the location of each character within the case and the quantity of each character. The work also highlights occasional mistakes on the part of those using the typecase, as the odd rogue letter crops up in the wrong location.

The first sheet acts as a 'road map' of the typecase, showing all the streets, avenues and back alleys of the structure. The case is printed in silver, with each character location denoted by a single black character. The following sheets show a variety of fonts from Helvetica Light 12pt to Grotesque No. 9 in 60pt. One sheet, which is dedicated to 'miscellaneous stock blocks', shows an eclectic mix of logos, illustrations and dingbats. Another page shows all six font sheets overprinted: Helvetica Light, Gill Sans Italic, Baskerville Roman, Fashion Script, Grotesque No. 9 and Joanna Roman are overlaid to create a dense cityscape of the collection. Finally, a set of three pages shows the reverse side of the three forms used on the job, which represent the complex infrastructure of the work.

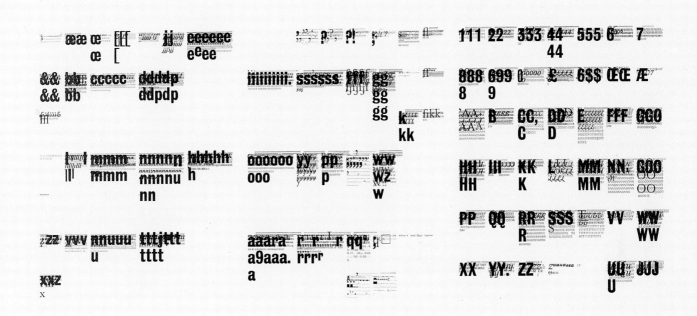

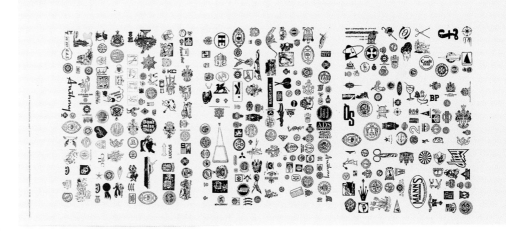

Design   Mark El-khatib
Project   European Atlas

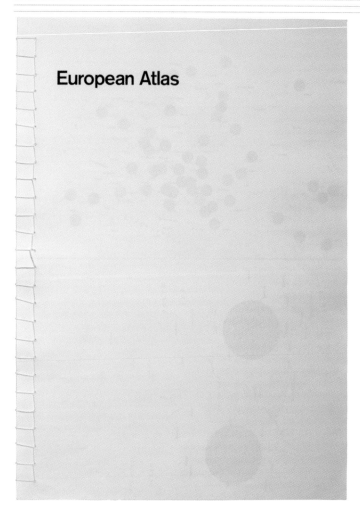

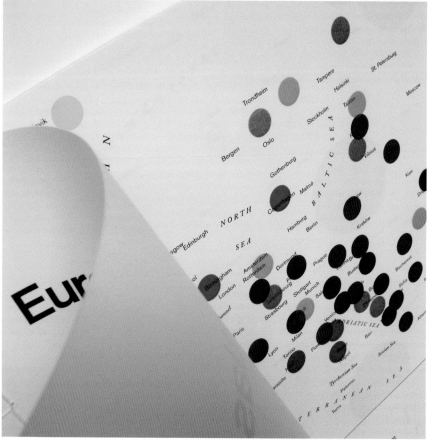

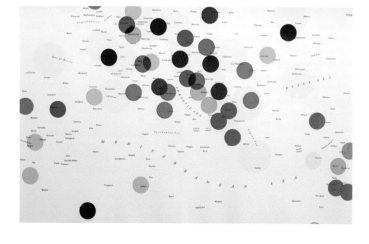

The brief for this final year degree project was to explore the notion of thresholds. Various levels of information were removed to produce the atlas. The lines that define a country's border have been replaced with colour-coded dots - the colour of each dot relating to the number of countries that border it. The size of each dot also changes depending on the scale of the page.

The typographic vernacular of the source material is kept in tact, with only cities, oceans and seas being labelled. The result blurs the boundaries between countries, resulting in a fresh perspective on European geography.

The 20-page atlas is 11½ x 16⅝in (292 x 410mm), hand-stitched and laser printed on paper that allows for lots of show-through.

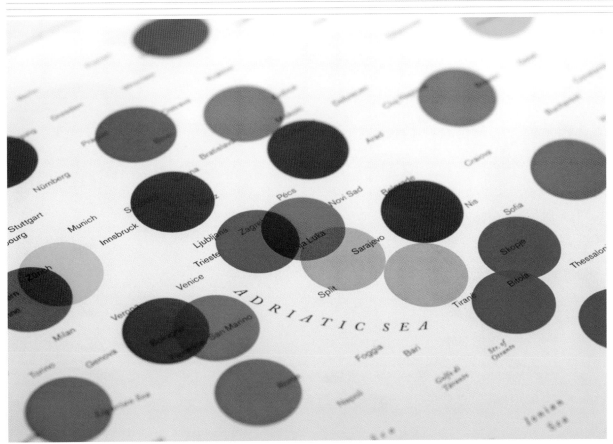

Design	Mark Diaper
Artist	Michael Landy
Project	Breakdown
Client	Artangel

BREAK DOWN

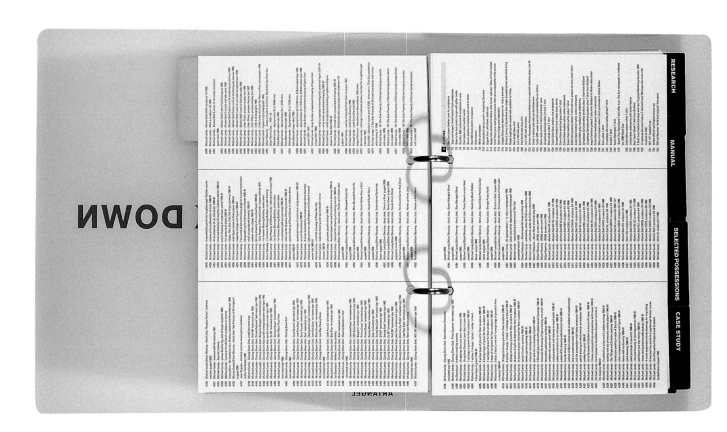

Over the course of two weeks in February 2001, the British artist Michael Landy took up residence in a former C&A clothing store in London's Oxford Street, and systematically destroyed all of his personal possessions, from his car to his passport and credit cards, in an industrial shredder. Prior to the event, the artist had made an inventory of his possessions – in effect, an inventory of his 37-year life. Over 5000 entries catalogued every piece of furniture, every record, every article of clothing, every letter from friends, every gadget, and every work of art – his own work and gifts from fellow artists such as Gary Hume – which were owned by the artist.

This inventory forms the basis of a book, designed by Mark Diaper, produced to document the project by Artangel, the agency which funded it. The possessions are categorised and given a prefix: A = Artworks, C = Clothing, E = Electrical, F = Furniture, K = Kitchen, L = Leisure, MV = Motor Vehicle, P = Perishables, R = Reading Materials, S = Studio Materials. When the destruction of the objects took place, they were loaded onto a complex conveyor belt system which fed four work bays, each dedicated to the dismantling of certain items identified by these prefixes.

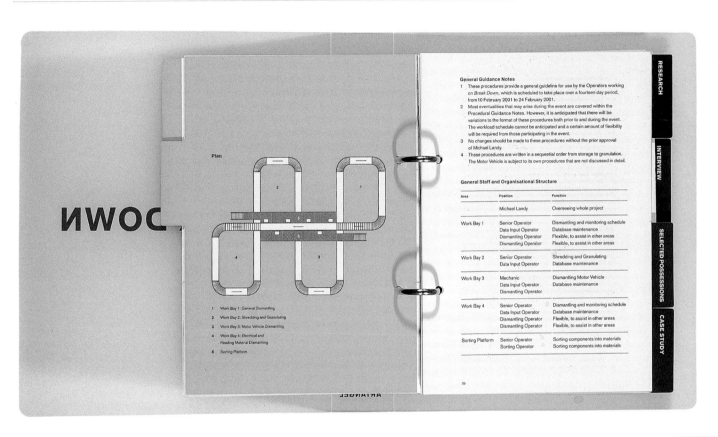

Design   Sans+Baum
Map design   Russell Bell
Project   Facts of Life gallery guide

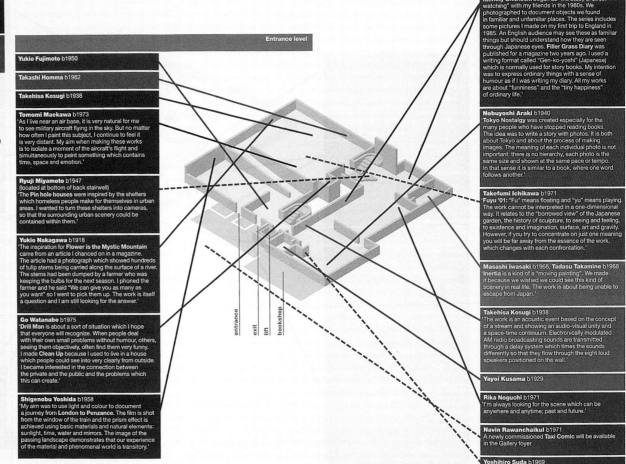

Hayward Gallery
on the South Bank · London

Facts of Life
Comtemporary Japanese art
Hayward Gallery
4 October – 9 December 2001

Facts of Life presents painting, photography, video, installation, sculpture, sound pieces and performance work – in the galleries, on the sculpture courts and outside – by 26 artists, all Japanese or working in Japan. It proposes links between established figures of an older generation and younger, emerging artists; all the work has been made in recent years, much of it especially for this exhibition.

The title – Facts of Life – points to a directness, an unmediated approach and a realism which unites all the work on show. The artists shown here, although their approaches differ widely, share an engagement with the real world: both with the minutiae of everyday experience and with the larger realities which govern our lives. This attitude – prevalent internationally – is in marked contrast to the academic and self-conscious postmodernism which characterised Japanese art in the 80s and 90s, and challenges the notion of Japan as a synthetic culture, an amalgam of virtual realities and wonderful fictions.

FACTS OF LIFE
for extended information on all the artists in Facts of Life log on to the special exhibition site at
www.haywardgallery.org.uk

Entrance level

Yukio Fujimoto b1950

Takashi Homma b1962

Takehisa Kosugi b1938

Tomomi Maekawa b1973
'As I live near an air base, it is very natural for me to see military aircraft flying in the sky. But no matter how often I paint this subject, I continue to feel it is very distant. My aim when making these works is to isolate a moment of the aircraft's flight and simultaneously to paint something which contains time, space and emotion.'

Ryuji Miyamoto b1947
(located at bottom of back stairwell)
'The **Pin hole houses** were inspired by the shelters which homeless people make for themselves in urban areas. I wanted to turn these shelters into cameras, so that the surrounding urban scenery could be contained within them.'

Yukio Nakagawa b1918
'The inspiration for **Flower is the Mystic Mountain** came from an article I chanced on in a magazine. The article had a photograph which showed hundreds of tulip stems being carried along the surface of a river. The stems had been dumped by a farmer who was keeping the bulbs for the next season. I phoned the farmer and he said "We can give you as many as you want" so I went to pick them up. The work is itself a question and I am still looking for the answer.'

Go Watanabe b1975
'**Drill Man** is about a sort of situation which I hope that everyone will recognize. When people deal with their own small problems without humour, others, seeing them objectively, often find them very funny. I made **Clean Up** because I used to live in a house which people could see into very clearly from outside. I became interested in the connection between the private and the public and the problems which this can create.'

Shigenobu Yoshida b1958
'My aim was to use light and colour to document a journey from **London to Penzance**. The film is shot from the window of the train and the prism effect is achieved using basic materials and natural elements: sunlight, time, water and mirrors. The image of the passing landscape demonstrates that our experience of the material and phenomenal world is transitory.'

entrance
exit
lift
bookshop

Genpei Akasegawa b1937
'**Identity Unknown** began as "the study of street watching" with my friends in the 1980s. We photographed to document objects we found in familiar and unfamiliar places. The series includes some pictures I made on my first trip to England in 1985. An English audience may see these as familiar things but should understand how they are seen through Japanese eyes. **Filler Grass Diary** was published for a magazine two years ago. I used a writing format called "Gen-ko-yoshi" (Japanese) which is normally used for story books. My intention was to express ordinary things with a sense of humour as if I was writing my diary. All my works are about "funniness" and the "tiny happiness" of ordinary life.'

Nobuyoshi Araki b1940
'**Tokyo Nostalgy** was created especially for the many people who have stopped reading books. The idea was to write a story with photos. It is both about Tokyo and about the process of making images. The meaning of each individual photo is not important: there is no hierarchy, each photo is the same size and shown at the same pace or tempo. In that sense it is similar to a book, where one word follows another.'

Takefumi Ichikawa b1971
'**Fuyu '01**: "Fu" means floating and "yu" means playing. The work cannot be interpreted in a one-dimensional way. It relates to the "borrowed view" of the Japanese garden, the history of sculpture, to seeing and feeling, to existence and imagination, surface, art and gravity. However, if you try to concentrate on just one meaning you will be far away from the essence of the work, which changes with each confrontation.'

Masashi Iwasaki b1966, **Tadasu Takamine** b1968
'**Inertia** is a kind of a "moving painting". We made it because we wished we could see this kind of scenery in real life. The work is about being unable to escape from Japan.'

Takehisa Kosugi b1938
'The work is an acoustic event based on the concept of a stream and showing an audio-visual unity and a space-time continuum. Electronically modulated AM radio broadcasting sounds are transmitted through a delay system which times the sounds differently so that they flow through the eight loud speakers positioned on the wall.'

Yayoi Kusama b1929

Rika Noguchi b1971
'I'm always looking for the scene which can be anywhere and anytime; past and future.'

Navin Rawanchaikul b1971
A newly commissioned **Taxi Comic** will be available in the Gallery foyer.

Yoshihiro Suda b1969

Produced as a concertina-folded sheet of paper, this gallery guide for the exhibition Facts of Life at the Hayward Gallery in London was designed to help visitors navigate easily around a fairly complex set of exhibits, while providing information about the artists whose works they encountered along the way. The primary intention was to design an accessible guide which made the different gallery levels and spaces immediately clear. A colour-coding system was introduced to draw attention to the individuality of each exhibitor and their work. The isometric drawings of the two levels of the gallery are annotated by thick rules colour-coded to identify the presence of particular artists' works, while dotted lines are used to indicate a work which occupies a non-standard gallery space such as the basement area or the gallery's foyer, for example.

Public programmes
An extensive programme of events gives adults, students and families a range of opportunities to engage with the issues and ideas behind Facts of Life. Gallery Guides are regularly on hand to offer short, informal tours of the exhibition and to answer your questions. A series of informal gallery talks by artists and curators is open to all, as well as our regular student debates, this time with Goldsmiths' College and Kingston University. Two Hayward Forums, and two seminars with the Institute of Ideas, present visitors with a chance to participate in inter-disciplinary discussions around identity, transience, globalisation and the myths of orientalism and universalism.

Families are invited to make pin-hole cameras, comic books and much more over the opening weekend with Takefumi Ichikawa and Ryuji Miyamoto, alongside British artists Sally Barker and Milika Muritu. In addition, artists will be leading workshops over the half-term holiday.

Full listings of Hayward Gallery events are given in the exhibition leaflet available in the foyer, or visit our website at www.haywardgallery.org.uk

Facts of Life catalogue
A fully illustrated catalogue accompanies the exhibition. The book includes texts by Jonathan Watkins and Mami Kataoka. The catalogue is available from the Hayward Shop at a special price during the exhibition, and by mail order from Cornerhouse Publications
telephone
+44 (0)161 200 1503

Disability access
For information on disability, please ask at the Information Point in the Hayward Gallery Foyer or
telephone
+44 (0)20 7960 5226
or
minicom textphone
+44 (0)20 7921 0921

selected by
Jonathan Watkins
co-organised by
The Hayward Gallery/
The Japan Foundation
support in-kind
All Nippon Airways
architectural design
David Dernie Architects
lighting design
Lightwaves
guide design
sans+baurh
guide diagrams
Russell Bell
guide texts
Artists' statements
copyright the artists
2001
guide print
Digital Brookdale

Co-organised with
 国際交流基金
The Japan Foundation
Supported in-kind by
ANA
 j ARTS COUNCIL sbc

Nobuyoshi Araki b1940
'I began photographing **Flowers** in the early 1970s at Jho-kan temple in Minowa where I grew up. Each year, during the weeks of the equinox, flowers were displayed in the temple. I would wait until these flowers started dying, then steal them and photograph them against a white background. For me, shooting fresh flowers is boring. I always wait until the flowers are dying because at that moment their eroticism and vitality is at its height. Flowers have became my abnormal love object.'

Yukio Fujimoto b1950
'The Philosphical Toys are simple objects made into musical boxes and designed to develop hearing ability and our relationship to simple things. **Cosmos (Black)** is about the balance of order and coincidence. The combination of spin and gravitation on the dice creates what seem like uneven sounds, but listen carefully, and you will realize that the sounds have a certain order. **Ears with Chair, Earpipes** were made at a time when my interest had changed from making sounds to listening to them.'

Tomoko Isoda b1976

Yayoi Kusama b1929
Narcissus Garden, was first made for the Venice Bienale in 1966. The 1,500 silver plastic spheres were placed in rows on a twenty metre square lawn in front of the Italian Pavilion. Kusama caused a sensation by selling the balls to passers-by for two dollars each, which at the time was seen as a radical gesture against the art market. In 1966 she said of the work: 'Artists should integrate themselves into economic life by making their work inexpensive and accessible enough to be bought like items in a supermarket'. For this showing the silver spheres are not for sale but the artist still maintains her stance: 'I will buy your narcissism for two dollars'.

Makoto Nomura b1968
2–9 November
Will be performing **Shogi** compositions in the Gallery.

Shimabuku b1969
'I took a living octopus that I had caught myself, to Tokyo. Then I brought it back, still alive, and returned it to the sea. This was probably the first octopus in history to go to Tsukiji, the big fish market in Tokyo, and come back alive. The octopus returned to the ocean in Akashi in good health. What does the octopus remember about this event? Is he talking to his fellow octopi at the bottom of the ocean about his trip to Tokyo? Or has he got inside an octopus trap with the idea that he might not be able to go to Tokyo again? In a way this was my Apollo project because taking an octopus to Tokyo is like taking humans to the moon.'

Tatsuo Miyajima b1957
'I am currently interested in exploring ideas of time and space through direct communication with the audience. In **Floating Time** numbers between one and nine appear suspended in space (zero is not included because it means death). The numbers express the rhythm of time and the lives of individual human beings. When people step into the work they transform it. The space ceases to be abstract and becomes real, animated and alive. Without an audience this work can never be complete.'

Ryuji Miyamoto b1947
'I began the series **Inside Out, Upside Down** because I found it interesting that the images I made using the **Pin hole houses** appeared as they did. Images are received upside down on the retina of the human eye, which is itself a form of camera. Looking at the photos helps us to recognize that the world we are seeing is always "relative".'

Rogues' Gallery: Yasuhiko Hamachi b1970, **Yukihisa Nakase** b1971
The environment which we occupy on a daily basis is full of hidden elements, things we are not always conscious of. We are interested in extracting that which is not immediately apparent in our daily lives and converting it into real experience. **Residual Noise** encourages the audience to rediscover the phenomenon of sound.

Shimabuku b1969

Hiroshi Sugimoto b1948
'Accelerated Buddha began as 48 photographs of the 1,000 Buddha figures at the Hall of Thirty-Three Bays in Kyoto. One after the other, these individual images were photographed on video. The video of the 48 photographs of the 1,000 Buddhas was then looped 100 times so when you watch this video you are meeting 100,000 Buddhas in a mere five minutes. The lithographs on the wall, **In Praise of Shadows**, were made by photographing with the camera's aperture open for the time it took for a candle to burn. As the evening breeze fluttered the flame, my camera collected the trace of light and time on its film. Maybe it has to do with making the visible invisible.'

Atsuko Tanaka b1932

Yuji Watabe b1974
'I use my drawing to document and express my personal memories. I draw on the wall because it is permanent. I want to transfer the memories on to the wall as fast as possible. It is essential that the girls on the wall are my friends because with these drawings I want to keep the moments which I have shared with these girls. Through the work, I want to the audience to experience the invisible: time.'

cafe

lift

Upper level

Design   Cartlidge Levene
Project   Selfridges Birmingham brochure
Architects   Future Systems

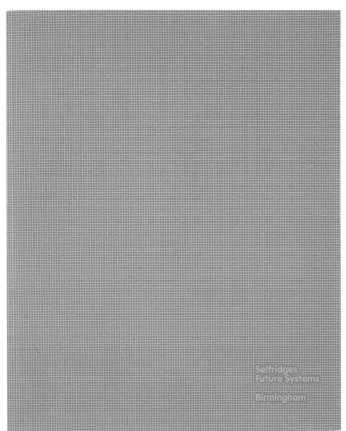

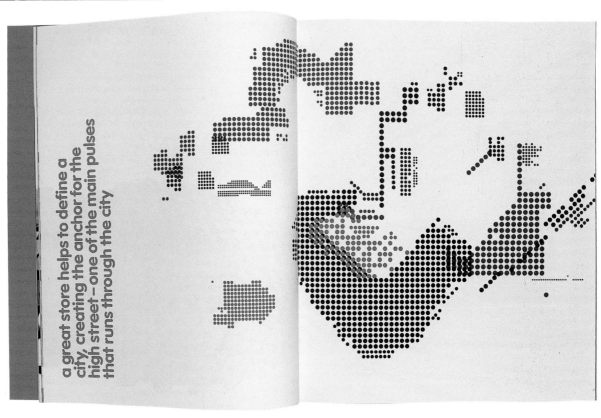

a great store helps to define a
city, creating the anchor for the
high street – one of the main pulses
that runs through the city

Selfridges department stores and the architectural firm Future Systems requested the help of the London-based design consultancy Cartlidge Levene to design a promotional brochure for a new Selfridges store to be opened in Birmingham. Targeted at fashion brand owners, who might open branded concessions in the store, the aim of the brochure was to generate interest in the as yet unbuilt Birmingham Selfridges. The brochure includes models by Future Systems showing the proposed new building, whose organic form is covered with circular discs. The motif is used throughout the brochure as a graphic device. The publication includes a map showing the customer catchment area in and around the city of Birmingham, demonstrating the potential of the area to investors, and making a graphic feature of further abstractions of the map in different colours.

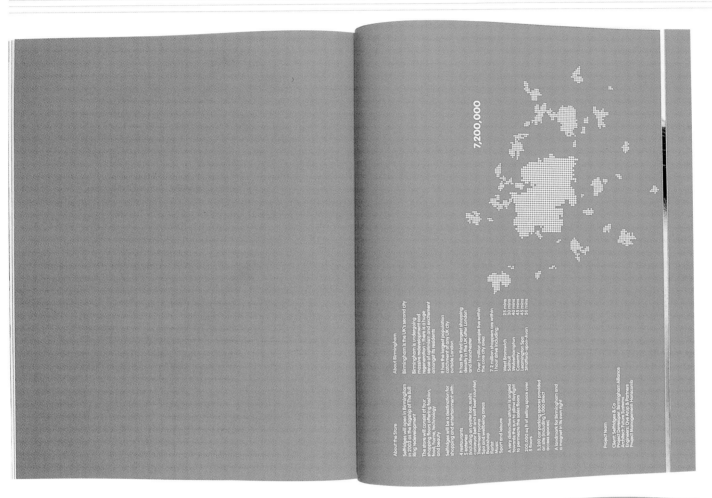

Design   Build
Project   'TRVL'

Build is a UK-based design consultancy established by Michael Place, who was previously employed at The Designers Republic. When he was commissioned by the Japanese graphic design journal Idea to produce a piece of work, he chose to base it on the 281-day round-the-world trip he had taken between leaving The Designers Republic and founding Build. The resulting piece is a supplement/book which acts as a travelogue – a graphic depiction of the journey.

'TRVL', as it was titled, is a 24-page French-folded publication featuring photographs taken during the trip, which are supported by and cross-referenced with location/map references and records of times and distances travelled. Each page represents a stage of the journey, identified by arrival and departure times and related data.

Design   Nick Thornton-Jones/Warren Du Preez
Project   Human mapping research project

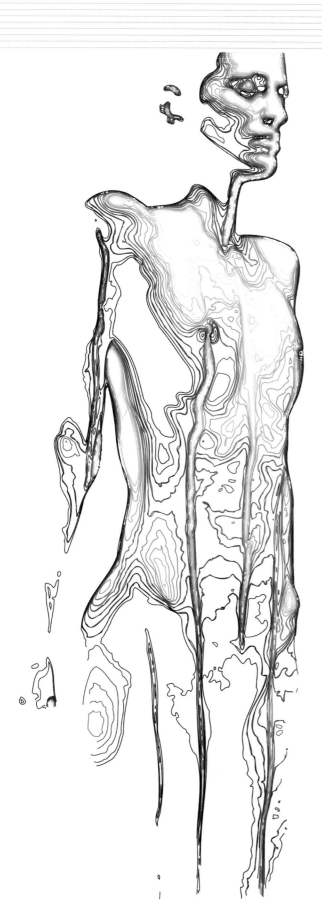

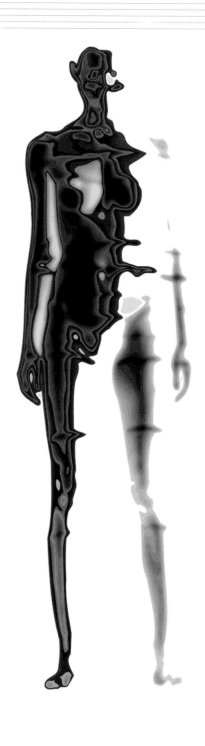

Nick Thornton-Jones and Warren Du Preez work together as image creators. With Du Preez coming from a fashion photography background and Thornton-Jones coming from graphic design and illustration, together they blur the boundaries between photography and digital illustration.

The work shown here is part of an ongoing research project into the abstraction and reduction of the human form into light and contours, exploring surface, curvature, volume and perspective. They are interested in discovering a point at which a photograph becomes a graphic representation, and how far this representation can be pushed. By reducing images of the body to a series of tonal contour lines, the pair explore a level of information about shape and form that is not normally evident – or at least given prominence – in representations of the human figure.

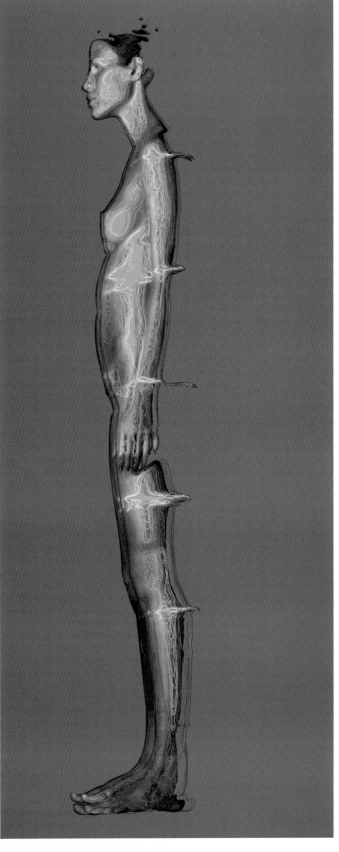

Studio   Sinutype
Design   Maik Stapelberg and Daniel Fritz
Project   'AM7/The Sun Years'

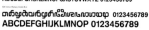

The 'Akademische Mitteilungen' (Academic Announcements) is a publication of the Academy of Arts and Design in Stuttgart, Germany. The magazine is published once a year by two graphic design students from the academy. The content of the magazine is always based around one main theme. The seventh issue of the magazine, designed by Daniel Fritz and Maik Stapelberg, was titled 'AM7'. The theme running throughout this issue was 'communication'.

The AM7 Sun Poster elaborates on an article written in the magazine called 'Sun Years', which is a fictional story about Elvis being kidnapped after an alien race listened to his music which was on the golden record sent on a Voyager probe in 1977. The poster, which measures 46²¹/₃₂ x 32⁷/₈in (1185 x 835mm), shows a series of very elaborate and stylistic maps for the fictional world 'Planet Roosta' whose continents bear a striking resemblance to a portrait of the King himself.

The poster forms a total graphic manual for Planet Roosta, showing everything from corporate colour palette and typeface to pharmaceutical and food packaging, and maps the entire infrastructure of the civiliasation. It includes a revised map of the solar system; a world map; a map of Sun Islands focusing on their roads, waterways and cities; a map of Wayon, the capital of North Alacarecca; a map of Sun, the capital of Sun Islands with a zoom-in Sun Downtown (Streetmap); and also a ferry map for Sun Island (shown below).

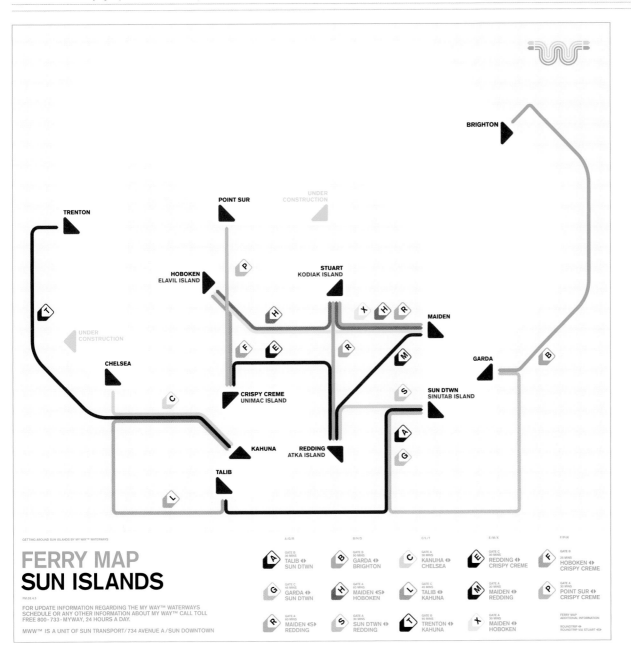

FERRY MAP
SUN ISLANDS

Studio   Sinutype
Design   Maik Stapelberg and Daniel Fritz
Project   'AM7/The Sun Years'

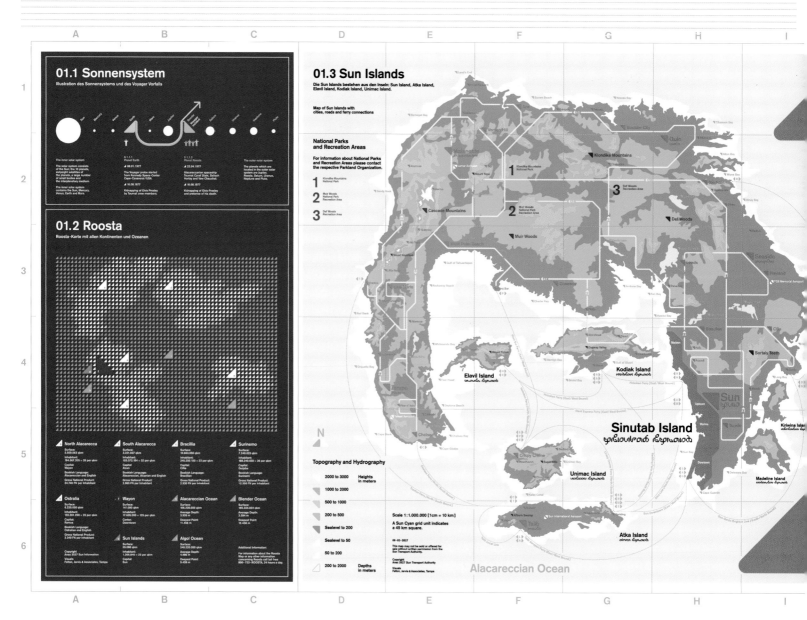

Shown here in more detail are: a revised map of the solar system; a world map; a map of Sun Islands focusing on its roads, waterways and cities; a map of Wayon, the capital of North Alacarecca; a map of Sun; and the capital of Sun Islands with a zoom-in Sun Downtown (Streetmap).

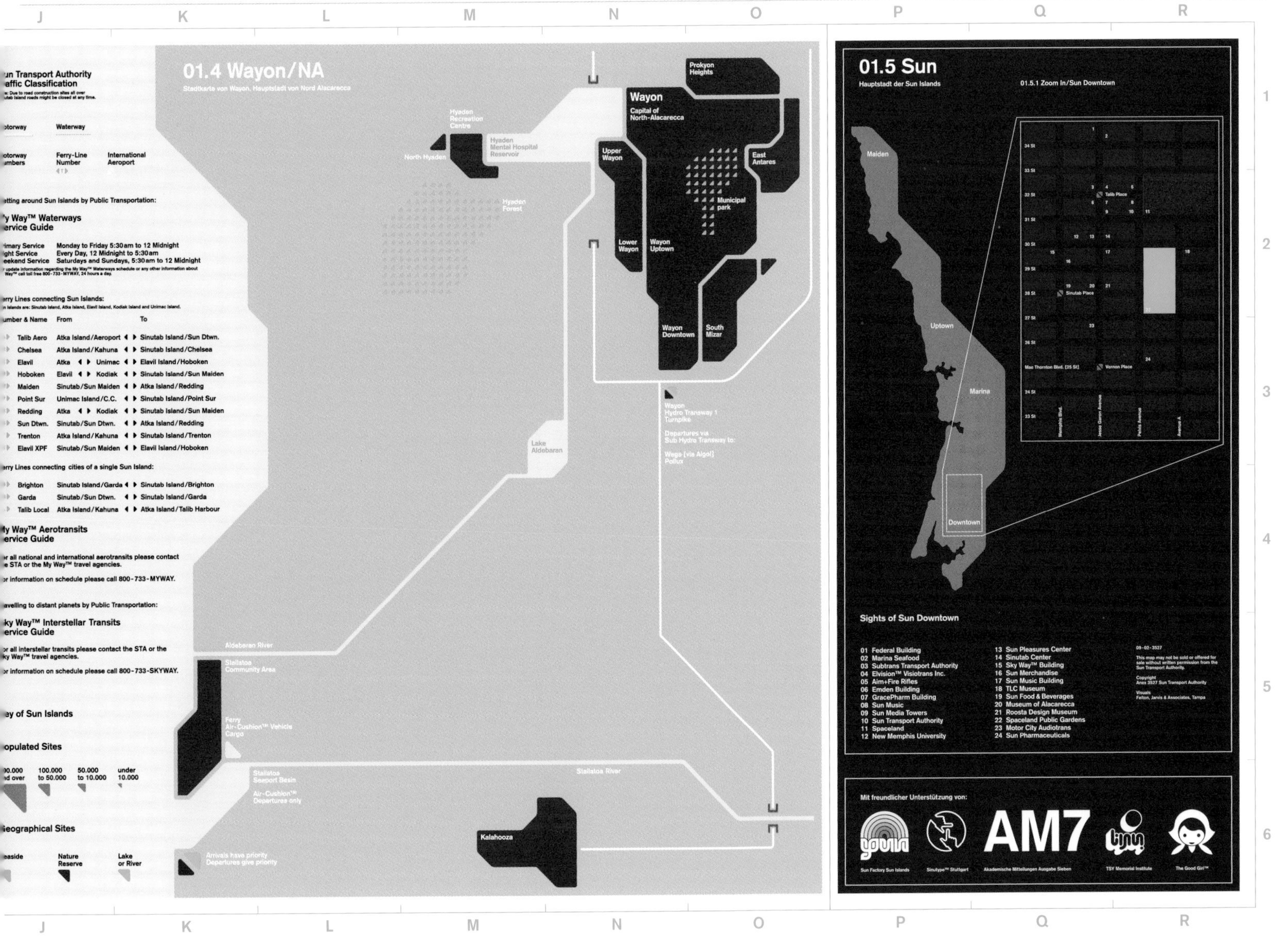

01.4 Wayon/NA
Stadtkarte von Wayon, Hauptstadt von Nord Alacarecca

**Sun Transport Authority
Traffic Classification**

Note: Due to road construction sites all over Sun Islands roads might be closed at any time.

Motorway	Waterway
Motorway Numbers	Ferry-Line Number	International Aeroport

Getting around Sun Islands by Public Transportation:

**My Way™ Waterways
Service Guide**

Primary Service	Monday to Friday 5:30am to 12 Midnight
Night Service	Every Day, 12 Midnight to 5:30am
Weekend Service	Saturdays and Sundays, 5:30am to 12 Midnight

For update information regarding the Sky Way™ Waterways schedule or any other information about My Way™ call toll free 800-733-MYWAY, 24 hours a day.

Ferry Lines connecting Sun Islands:

Sun Islands are: Sinutab Island, Atka Island, Elavil Island, Kodiak Island and Unimac Island.

Number & Name	From		To
Talib Aero	Atka Island/Aeroport	◀▶	Sinutab Island/Sun Dtwn.
Chelsea	Atka Island/Kahuna	◀▶	Sinutab Island/Chelsea
Elavil	Atka ◀▶ Unimac	◀▶	Elavil Island/Hoboken
Hoboken	Elavil ◀▶ Kodiak	◀▶	Sinutab Island/Sun Maiden
Maiden	Sinutab/Sun Maiden	◀▶	Atka Island/Redding
Point Sur	Unimac Island/C.C.	◀▶	Sinutab Island/Point Sur
Redding	Atka ◀▶ Kodiak	◀▶	Sinutab Island/Sun Maiden
Sun Dtwn.	Sinutab/Sun Dtwn.	◀▶	Atka Island/Redding
Trenton	Atka Island/Kahuna	◀▶	Sinutab Island/Trenton
Elavil XPF	Sinutab/Sun Maiden	◀▶	Elavil Island/Hoboken

Ferry Lines connecting cities of a single Sun Island:

Brighton	Sinutab Island/Garda	◀▶	Sinutab Island/Brighton
Garda	Sinutab/Sun Dtwn.	◀▶	Sinutab Island/Garda
Talib Local	Atka Island/Kahuna	◀▶	Atka Island/Talib Harbour

**My Way™ Aerotransits
Service Guide**

For all national and international aerotransits please contact the STA or the My Way™ travel agencies.

For information on schedule please call 800-733-MYWAY.

Travelling to distant planets by Public Transportation:

**Sky Way™ Interstellar Transits
Service Guide**

For all interstellar transits please contact the STA or the Sky Way™ travel agencies.

For information on schedule please call 800-733-SKYWAY.

Key of Sun Islands

Populated Sites

100.000 and over	100.000 to 50.000	50.000 to 10.000	under 10.000

Geographical Sites

Seaside	Nature Reserve	Lake or River

Prokyon Heights

Wayon
Capital of
North-Alacarecca

Hyaden Recreation Centre

Hyaden Mental Hospital Reservoir

North Hyaden

Hyaden Forest

Upper Wayon

East Antares

Municipal Park

Lower Wayon

Wayon Uptown

Wayon Downtown

South Mizar

Wayon Hydro Transway 1 Turnpike

Departures via Sub Hydro Transway to:

Wega (via Algol)
Pollux

Lake Aldebaran

Aldebaran River

Stellatoo Community Area

Ferry Air-Cushion™ Vehicle Cargo

Stellatoo Seaport Basin

Air-Cushion™ Departures only

Stellatoo River

Kalahooza

Arrivals have priority Departures give priority

01.5 Sun
Hauptstadt der Sun Islands   01.5.1 Zoom In/Sun Downtown

Maiden

Uptown

Marina

Downtown

34 St
33 St
32 St
31 St
30 St
29 St
28 St
27 St
26 St
25 St
24 St
23 St

Talib Place
Sinutab Place
Max Thornton Blvd. [35 St]
Vernon Place

Sights of Sun Downtown

01	Federal Building	13	Sun Pleasures Center
02	Marina Seafood	14	Sinutab Center
03	Subtrans Transport Authority	15	Sky Way™ Building
04	Elvision™ Visiotrans Inc.	16	Sun Merchandise
05	Aim+Fire Rifles	17	Sun Music Building
06	Emden Building	18	TLC Museum
07	GracePharm Building	19	Sun Food & Beverages
08	Sun Music	20	Museum of Alacarecca
09	Sun Media Towers	21	Roosta Design Museum
10	Sun Transport Authority	22	Spaceland Public Gardens
11	Spaceland	23	Motor City Audiotrans
12	New Memphis University	24	Sun Pharmaceuticals

09-02-3527

This map may not be sold or offered for sale without written permission from the Sun Transport Authority.

Copyright
Anno 3527 Sun Transport Authority

Visuals
Felton, Jarvis & Associates, Tampa

Mit freundlicher Unterstützung von:

Sun Factory Sun Islands   Sinutype™ Stuttgart   **AM7**   Akademische Mitteilungen Ausgabe Sieben   TSY Memorial Institute   The Good Girl™

Studio   Sinutype
Design   Maik Stapelberg and Daniel Fritz
Project   AM7/File Exchange

text: nadia abou-aly

With the File Exchange, another project for AM7,
Fritz and Stapelberg wanted to create a spontaneous,
communicative event paying tribute to the concepts
of mail-art. They built a network of 14 graphic design
groups from different countries and cities using mass
media (Internet), to interact/collaborate on a given
subject (what does communication mean to you?),
thereby creating a collective-visual work in a
unpredictable way which – in the final viewing – is as
surprising to the participants as it is to the viewer.
Contributors to the File Exchange project included Norm,
Lahm, joergbauerdesign and Peter Stemmler (eboy).

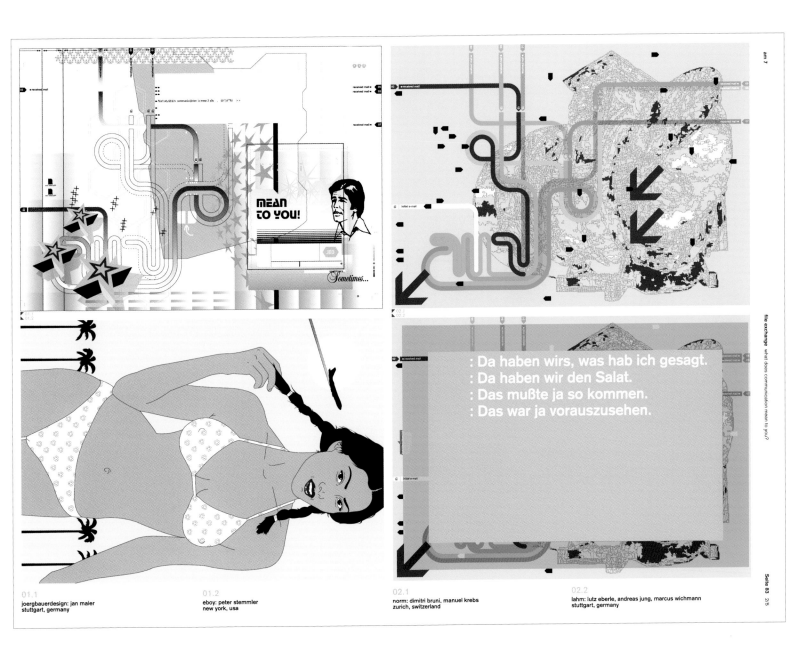

01.1
joergbauerdesign: jan maier
stuttgart, germany

01.2
eboy: peter stemmler
new york, usa

02.1
norm: dimitri bruni, manuel krebs
zurich, switzerland

02.2
lahm: lutz eberle, andreas jung, marcus wichmann
stuttgart, germany

Design   Lust
Project   Lust Map

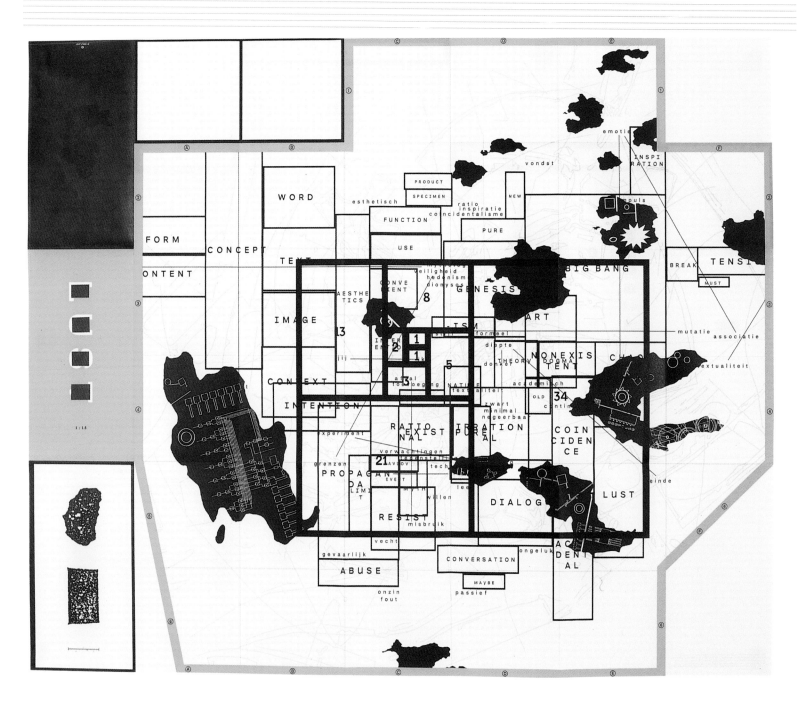

This map functions as a conceptual guide to the inner workings of the studio that designed it, Lust. It was created as a map to accompany two separate design projects, one being a study of the role of coincidence and association in graphic design, and the other being the implementation of these concepts in relation to architecture and urban structures. According to the designers, the key elements of the map which directly relate to the Lust design philosophy and methodology include an associative collection of words, a ratio of magnification, a virtual legend, a relative scale, an index of self-defined words and images, coincidental spaces, architectural and urban structures, the Golden Section, Fibonacci numbers, an intentionally broken piece of glass, a black square, and a pin-up girl.

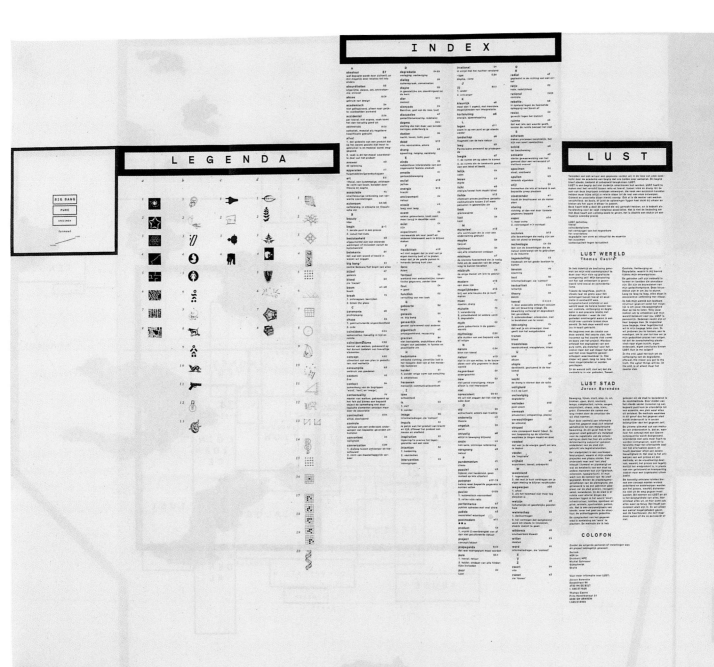

Design   Browns
Project   '0°'
Photography   John Wildgoose

Produced in time for the Millennium celebrations at the end of 1999, '0°' is a beautifully produced book showing the work of the photographer John Wildgoose. The book follows the Greenwich Meridian as it passes through England, from Peacehaven in the south to Tunstall in the north. The line, which represents the Prime Meridian of the world – 0° longitude – dictates that every place on earth is measured in terms of its distance east or west of it. From rolling chalk hills to flatlands, the images are held together by that invisible man-made thread which circles the world. Images were taken directly north or south along the 0° line. Nothing was chosen for its particular beauty or ugliness, and nothing was shot for political reasons. The only arbiter was the line.

02_Inhabitable space

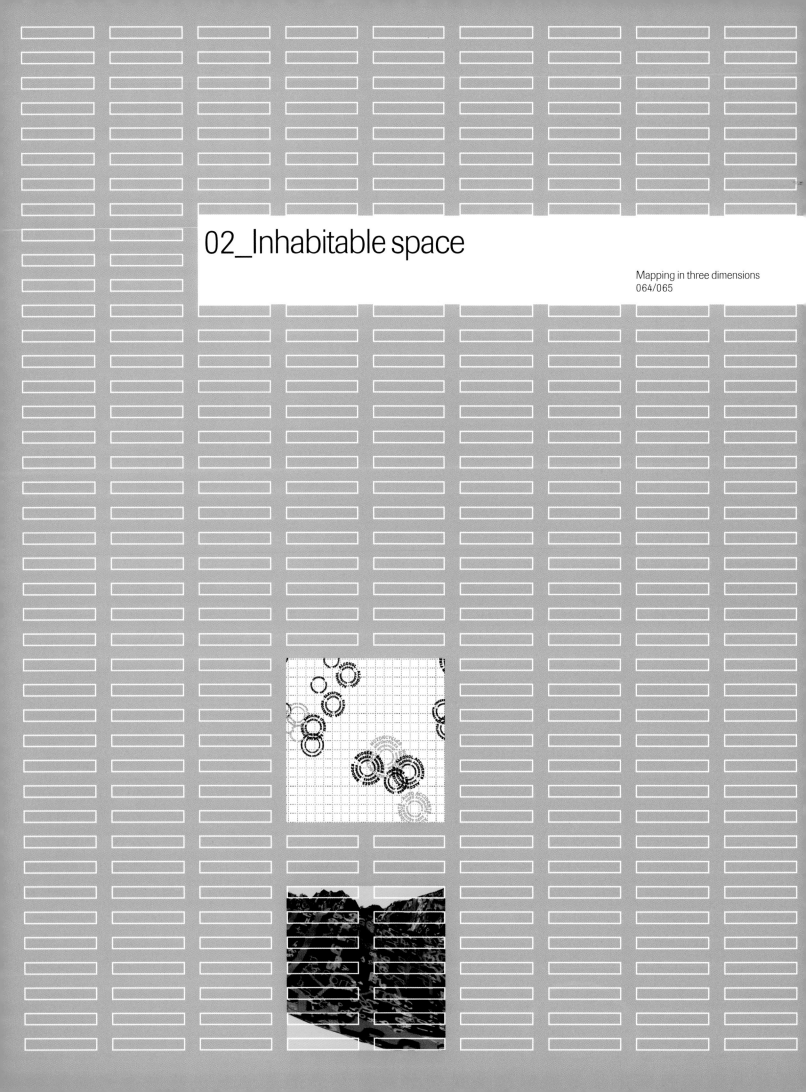

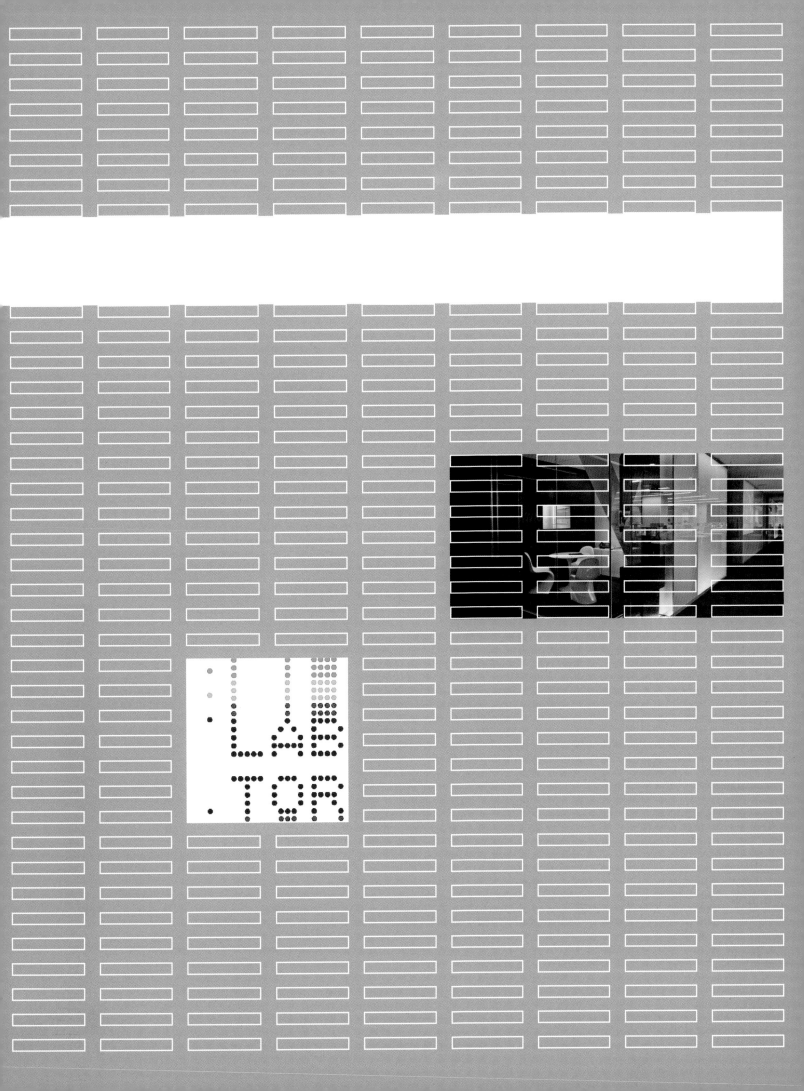

LAB
TOR

The inhabitable map

Essay by William Owen + Fenella Collingridge
066/067

The dividing line between the map, the landscape and the narratives scored onto it by man can be very slim. Subject and object have a tendency to intersect and fuse, each influencing the other. Before humans made maps they incised them on the landscape – both small signs and megamaps marking out territory or homestead, naming places and objects and providing orientation. The handheld map, whether made of stone, papyrus or paper, comes much later.

Man-made marks on the landscape have large ambitions: they tell narratives of life and death and attempt to control and moderate nature. There are numerous examples of these megamappings at huge scale still in existence. The Egyptian necropolis plots the path to the underworld; the giant neolithic chalk figures in southern England proclaim fertility and virility; the intaglio geoglyphs (incised pictures) in Blythe, California, are barely visible from the ground but vast when seen from the air. Another example would be the extraordinary Nazca lines in Peru which are believed to be a model at a huge scale of the drainage from the Andes mountains into the Nazca desert, with ceremonial walkways travelled by the map's makers to encourage the water down.

We have our modern equivalents in art, architecture and engineering of people's attempts to feel as large as the landscape they inhabit. The artist Christo wrapped in fabric (and remade) whole coastlines and photographed them from the air. In the United States the National Survey and Land Acts have recreated the literal appearance of a map on the surface of the western states, marked out in the chequerboard landscape of 1-mile squares created by fields and roads that religiously follow the survey lines. This repetitious, hyper-rationalist grid deviates only to pass insurmountable natural obstacles such as rivers, canyons or mountain ranges. Here is a case of the mapmakers not merely recording the landscape, but subjugating it, however imperfectly.

The modern city, too, is subtly and not so subtly marked in many hundreds of ways by objects, signs and symbols that exist only to map it and help us read the way. We insert small clues throughout the built environment to enable identification and orientation in cultural and geographical matters. Church spires and skyscrapers over-reach sight lines and provide orientation and locus; textured curbstones mark the boundary between road and walkway; signs identify buildings and their purpose or ownership; brass studs set into the pavement delineate property boundaries; viewpoints along major routes relate goal to starting point; and different districts are identified by their unique building types. These visual and textural cues are like a trail left by a pathfinder, clues to help us in our quest of navigation and exploration. We only register their importance where a city or suburb is visually homogenous, perhaps because – like Tokyo, for example – there are only one or two discernible historical layers, or because we are unfamiliar with the cultural signs of difference. The result is disorientation.

Every city and every district contains key modes of outlet or entry, often subway stations or rail termini, portals at which orientation is a critical issue and which establish the city's rhythm. Rational signage systems are built around these points, providing the text and directional markers that complete the inhabitable map.

Signage is a complex subset of information design that combines architectural, graphic and industrial design skills with a cartographer's understanding of theme. One signage system cannot serve every user. Some users may be visitors, with little knowledge of the city; others may be residents, familiar with the overall pattern but not the detail of certain districts. Some users will want to stay; others only want to leave. Some users may be travelling rapidly by car or bicycle, others by foot. Some users will be interested only in tourist sites, others in utilities like hospitals or transport. There are, clearly, only a limited number of themes, modes of passage and user goals that can be served by a single signage system before it overloads and collapses under its own weight.

Knowledge of a navigator's identity, location and intention is the holy grail of signage designers but something that in reality they can make only crude assumptions about.

Intégral Ruedi Baur
et Associés
Parc et Musée
Archéologique de
Kalkriese
092/093

Peter Anderson
Poles of Influence
096/097

Lust
Open Ateliers
2000
084/085

Knowledge of a navigator's identity, location and intention is the holy grail of signage designers but something that in reality they can make only crude assumptions about. If we were to make the ideal sign or map, we would know these things. And likewise, we would reintegrate the inhabitable three-dimensional landscape with the two-dimensional map so that they became one thing.

Digital technology brings us much nearer to the reintegration of sign, map and landscape, in the form of the mobile phone. Third generation mobile technology is not only capable of downloading video and cartographic data, but it is also location-sensitive, knows the identity of the user, and may through customisation or personalisation know or infer specific intentions at any one point in time.

Geographic Information Systems offer the potential to enable mobile phone users to interrogate objects, buildings – even people – or any selected thematic layer within the landscape (each will carry attribute data located at a specific logical address in the digital space that parallels its real address in the physical landscape), to push or pull information about events, services, times or offers at the user as well, of course, as acting as a traditional pictorial map.

Digital production, reproduction and distribution has exciting (and dreadful) implications for the way we make and use maps, and for the effect on the landscape maps survey.

First of all, we may no longer be using shared maps – as are the thousands of identical multiple-run printed maps – but ones that are unique to ourselves, with levels of access to information and control over the space of the city that varies according to all sorts of factors such as our personal selection, our credit card status, our phone company or our technical ability. Individuals may develop radically different viewpoints on the same location.

Secondly, the digital map may also map its user (the map knows its own location) and so there is the obvious possibility that a map of map-readers can be created, shifting constantly in real time as the readers move about. Feedback effects can result, as the world that is mapped changes according to the action of individuals responding to the map. This happens in printed maps too, but more slowly (the guide book recommends a restaurant, which as a result becomes overcrowded and therefore undesirable).

These feedback effects might create interesting and bizarre situations in a world in which we can survey, reproduce and distribute maps of the landscape instantaneously (mapping in real time). The flocking effect of in-car navigation systems, whereby the more cars that use the system and take similar congestion avoidance action, the more quickly alternative centres of congestion are created, is a prototypical example.

Real time mapping (using the appropriate sensors) enables us to map many new classes of object including those (like map readers) that are impermanent and highly localised: goods for sale, in storage or transit, for example; vehicles on the road; events; discarded items; pollution; weather. Knowledge of these things will affect their properties and relationships with each other and us. One can envisage that the overall effect could be a massive acceleration of change and a huge concentration of power and therefore value in the map. It is worth remembering, then, that in the Renaissance a map cost the equivalent of many thousands of times what it does today. The real time, location-aware, identity-aware, intention-aware maps of tomorrow may be equally valuable to their users.

Man-made marks on the landscape have large ambitions: they attempt to control and moderate nature.

Design   Projekttriangle
Project   Krypthästhesie

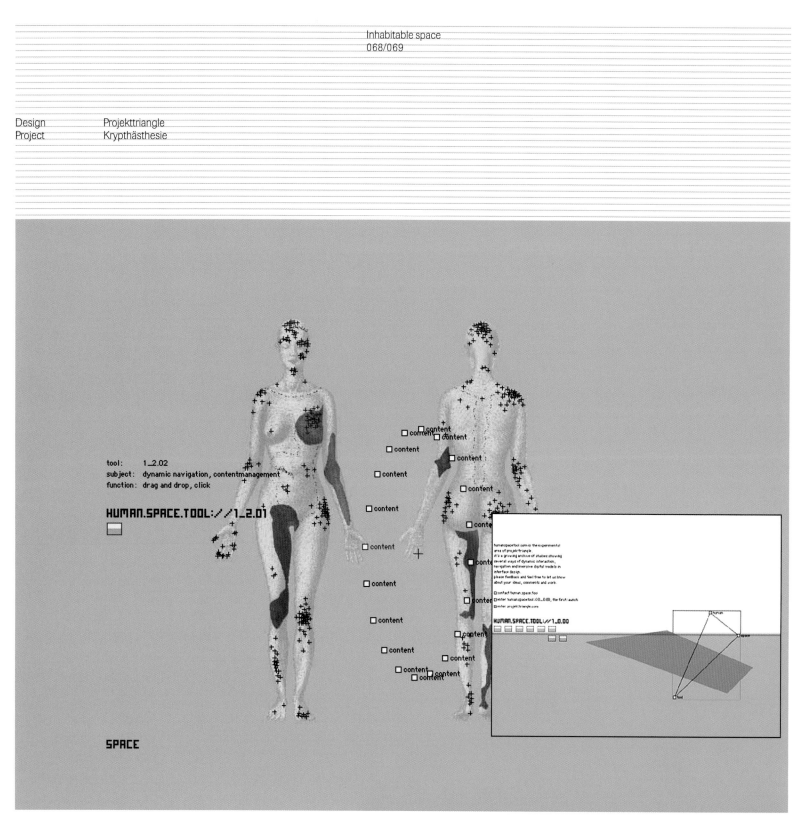

tool: 1_2.02
subject: dynamic navigation, contentmanagement
function: drag and drop, click

HUMAN.SPACE.TOOL://1_2.01

SPACE

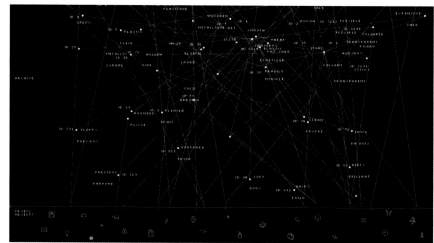

The mapping system Krypthästhesie was developed from German design company Projekttriangle's researches into a new and more effective way of finding and presenting information concealed in the multiplicity of data. "Our study is years ahead of the technology needed to implement it," says Martin Grothmaak of Projekttriangle. "We don't wait with our designs for the engineering to be available to put them into practice. What interests us is not the media themselves but intermedia relationships, in particular the inter-relationships between man and medium. Human beings are always at the centre of our interface design."

This research tool looks for information in big databases or on the Internet, evaluates it and displays it geometrically. The dynamic model illustrates both the content-based relationships between search criteria and the generation of search results. The results appear not as a list but as data clouds in the form of points in a circle around the central search word. If you search for information about 'Japan', for example, all the available information on that country appears as points distributed in a circle. A dynamic data map is created on the surface which permits a geographical orientation. The points closest to the search word contain a lot of information about Japan and the more distant ones less. If a second word – 'museums' – is entered at the edge of the circle the points rearrange themselves dynamically. They move towards the word to which they are most closely related. The user can now look at a point in more detail that is close to the word 'museums' but relatively far from 'Japan'. The information revealed when one clicks on the point turns out to be a museum of ethnology with Japanese exhibits.

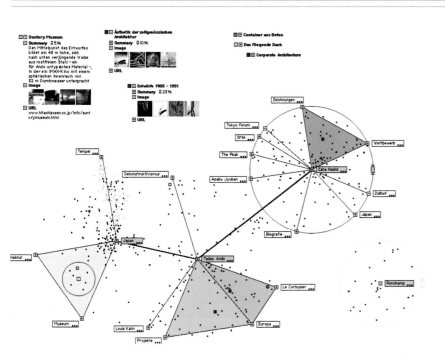

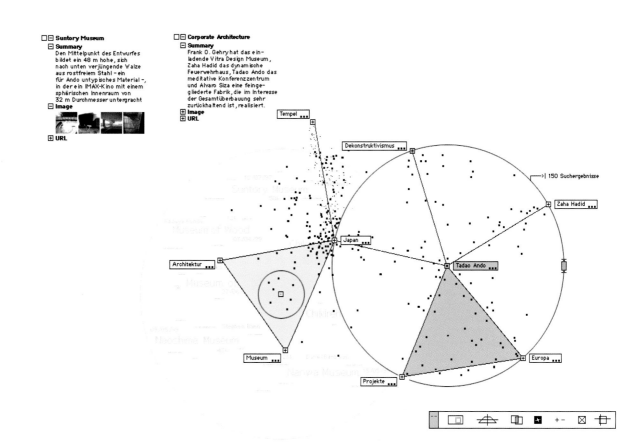

Design   Lust
Project   Atelier HSL web site

ATELIER
HSL

WAT IS
ATELIER
HSL
sla over

EEN KUNST- EN
URPR
GRAM A RO D
DE
HOG HEID
SLIJN-ZUID
sla over

EE KUNST-
EN CULTUUR-
PROGRAMMA
RO D DE
HOGESNELHEID
SLI N-ZUID
sla over

DE
SN
sla over

ATELIER HSL IS
EEN LABORATO-
RIUM EN KATA-
LYSATOR VOOR
CULTURELE PRO-
JECTEN ROND DE
HSL. IN DIT
LABORATORIUM
sla over

VINDT ONDER-
ZOEK PLAATS
NAAR DE CUL-
TURELE EN
MAATSCHAPPE-
LIJKE BETE-
KENIS
sla over

VAN DE HOGE-
SNELHEIDS-
LIJN EN HET
TOEKOMSTIGE
GEBRUIK
ERVAN.
sla over

Dit gebeurt door middel van het
geven van opdrachten aan kun-
stenaars, het organiseren van
tentoonstellingen en symposia
en het publiceren van uitgaven.
Maar Atelier HSL staat ook
open voor ideeën en concepten
van anderen. Atelier HSL ont-
wikkelt activiteiten voor een
sla over

publiek: (toekomstige) reizi-
gers, geïnteresseerden, en
omwonenden langs het tracé
van de hogesnelheidslijn, pro-
fessionals en liefhebbers uit de
wereld van kunst en
cultuur.nenden langs het tracé
van de hogesnelheidslijn, pro-
fessionals en liefhebbers uit de
wereld van kunst en cultuur.
sla over

sla over

WAT IS DE
CULTURELE
IMPACT
VAN DE HSL
LIJN
sla over

De HSL-Zuid verbindt
Nederland in 2006 met het
Europese net van hogesnel-
heidslijnen. De lijn doorsnijdt
en transformeert het door
mensenhanden aangelegde
polderlandschap en beïnvloedt
het stedelijke landschap. De
HSL levert een bijdrage aan
sla over

sla over

sla over

sla over

sla over

Het bijna 100 kilometer lange
tracé loopt dwars door
Nederland en telt tal van
'kunstwerken'. Bruggen, via-
ducten en tunnels vormen een
aaneenschakeling van monu-
menten van moderne techno
sla over

Evenzo omvangrijk en
indrukwekkend is de
ingreep die in de ruim-
telijke, maatschappelijk
en logistieke omgeving
van de lijn plaatsvindt.
sla over

sla over

sla.over

sla over

sla over

sla.over

BEKIJK EEN
INTERAC-
TIEVE VER-
BEELDING
sla over

sla over

sla over

sla over

sla over

DE HOGESNEL-
H NEN
VORME
S RARS T
F SIE N
C EL
INTERNET VAN
EUROPA.
sla over

sla over

SITE

Atelier HSL is an arts and cultural programme based around the Dutch High Speed Rail Line. Its web site functions as a medium where activities surrounding HSL are presented on-line. The concept for the interface is a matrix of points that symbolises points on a map and the distance between them. Since the arrival of the HSL, time and distance have become relative because of speed. Cities are drawn closer together: to a traveller, Amsterdam will be 'nearer' to Paris than to a southern Dutch city such as Maastricht. By the expansion and contraction of the points of the matrix, areas are created for the content of the site. This expansion and contraction relates back to the idea of the relativity of time and distance.

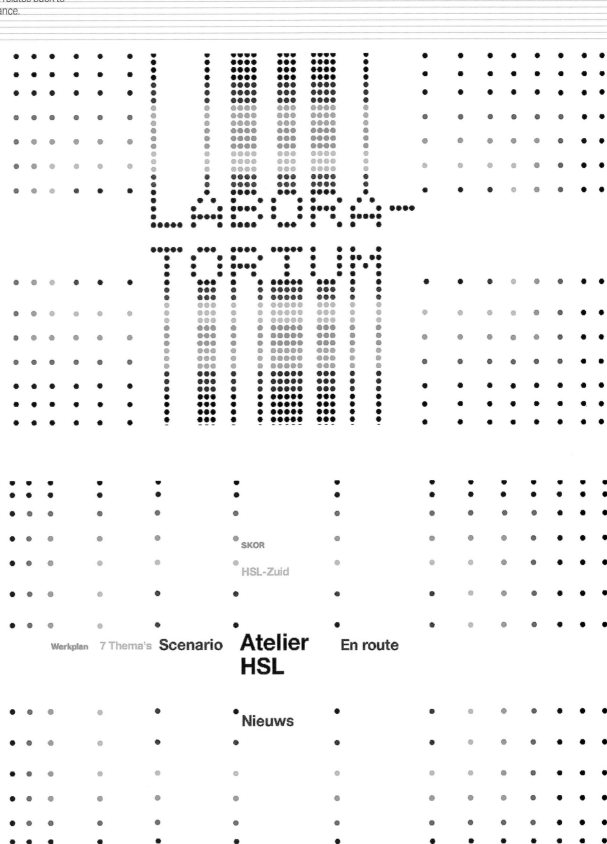

SKOR

HSL-Zuid

Werkplan   7 Thema's   Scenario   **Atelier HSL**   En route

Nieuws

Design   Cartlidge Levene
Project   Process type movie

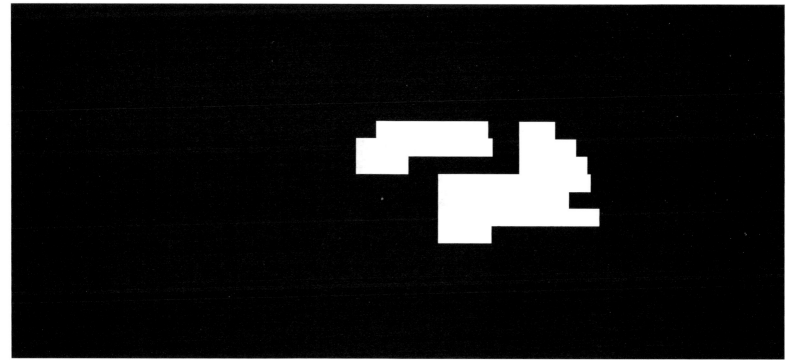

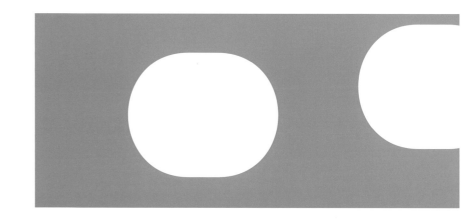

With no brief, apart from that the design company wished to be represented by an on-screen piece of work in an exhibition organised by the International Society of Typographic Designers held in London, Cartlidge Levene created the design shown here. The content of the seven-minute on-screen loop was created directly from dialogue around the subject of what the piece may become – a representation of conversation, over time, using typography and sound. The animated typography highlights structures and links though the repetition of words. Letters are repeated, removed and distorted during the loop.

— one thing I
to   , so it's not
just   , but,

be bad
— I can just imagine. things?

Design   Tomato Interactive
Project   Sony Vaio interface

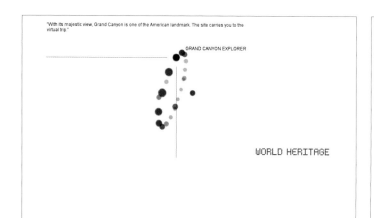

"With its majestic view, Grand Canyon is one of the American landmark. The site carries you to the virtual trip."

GRAND CANYON EXPLORER

WORLD HERITAGE

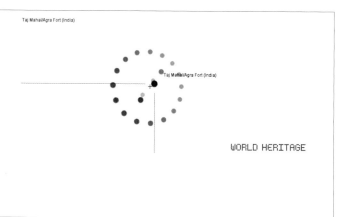

Taj Mahal/Agra Fort (India)

Taj Mahal/Agra Fort (India)

WORLD HERITAGE

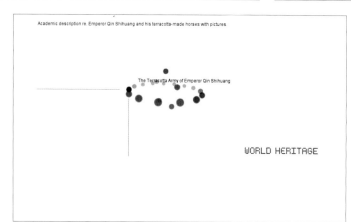

Academic description re. Emperor Qin Shihuang and his terracotta-made horses with pictures.

The Terracotta Army of Emperor Qin Shihuang

WORLD HERITAGE

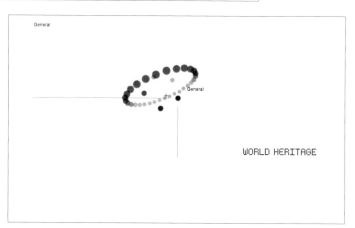

General

General

WORLD HERITAGE

Developed as an interface for the Sony Vaio system,
Tomato Interactive produced this on-screen navigational
world, in which the viewer can click on a morphic blob
and be transferred to another location and culture.
Despite containing a huge wealth of information, the
system is straightforward and simple to interact with.

"A monk visited eight sacred places for Buddhist, and writes up about the travel. Included here are
topics about Buddha, Gandhi, and Taj Mahal."

Road to Buddha

WORLD HERITAGE

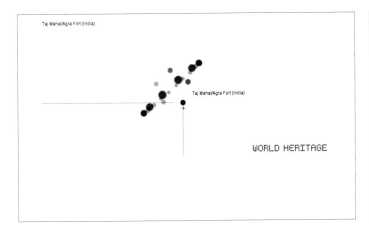

Taj Mahal/Agra Fort (India)

Taj Mahal/Agra Fort (India)

WORLD HERITAGE

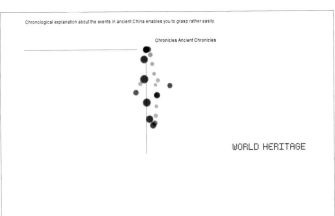

Chronological explanation about the events in ancient China enables you to grasp rather easily.

Chronicles Ancient Chronicles

WORLD HERITAGE

Design   City ID and Cartlidge Levene
Project   NewcastleGateshead QuayLink electric transit service
             and WalkRide information system

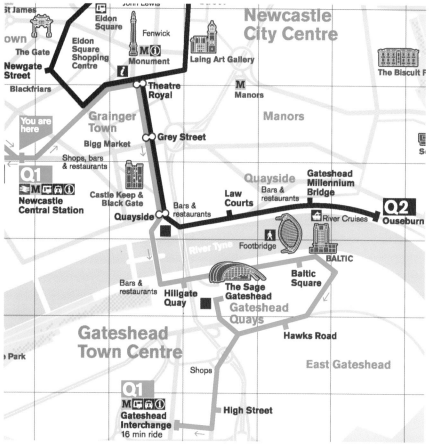

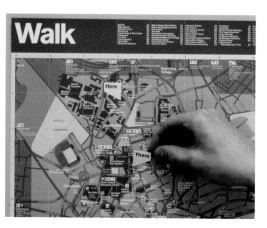

Newcastle City Council commissioned City ID to assess the measures required to meet the growing demands of visitors to the area. The information concept and identity, developed by City ID in partnership with Cartlidge Levene, led to the design of a world-class transit and information system targeted to the specific needs of tourists and visitors to NewcastleGateshead.

The system integrates the QuayLink transit system with pedestrian wayfinding and other information services to promote walking and public transport. City ID and Cartlidge Levene aimed to create a visual identity that captured the spirit of the city and provide a robust and unique set of elements to build upon throughout the design process.

The mapping information is designed to reflect the direction of travel. The design team worked closely with illustrator Russell Bell to create a simplified map base that illustrates how the QuayLink system connects key areas, destinations and transport interchanges in the city, allowing for people to plan their whole journey whether walking or riding.

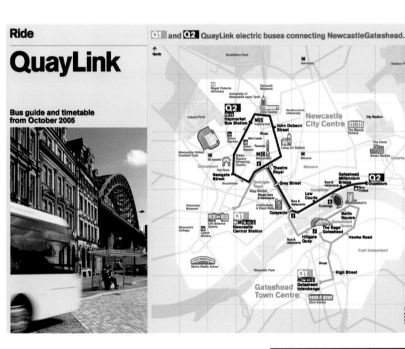

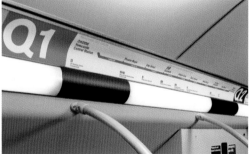

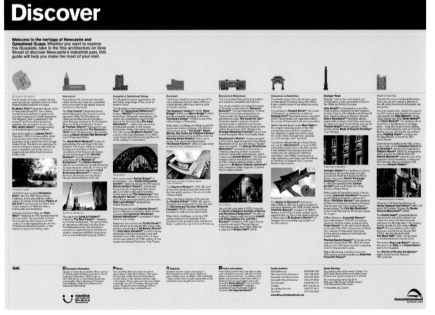

Design	City ID, Dalton Maag, Wood & Wood Signs and Endpoint
Project	Southampton Legible City

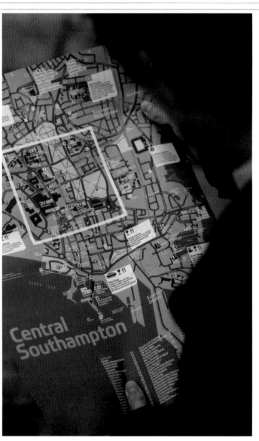

Southampton City Council had a vision to create a unique and dynamic voice to communicate clearly to visitors, businesses and residents, and promote walking and cycling as part of an active lifestyle.

City ID were commissioned to develop the Legible City concept, starting with a unique visual identity that included the design of a bespoke family of typefaces and pictogram set, developed with Dalton Maag.

A printed map was designed to illustrate both the key areas of the city and, in more detail, the central shopping area. A pilot wayfinding system, developed with Endpoint and manufactured by Wood & Wood, followed to include area maps and a city centre diagram designed to help orientate and reveal hotspots in the city. Illustrated by Russell Bell, the maps are simplified to promote walking routes, and include containers that provide information on where to eat, drink, shop or relax in the city – including how long it takes to walk there and how many calories will be burnt. The system is now being further extended across the rest of the city.

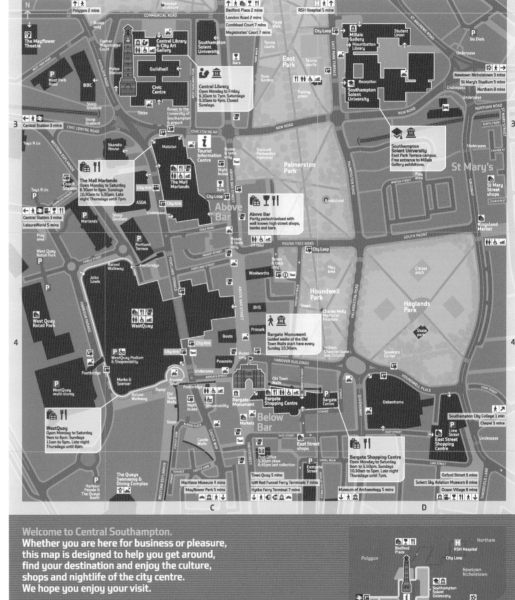

Design   City ID, Atelier Works and Pearson Lloyd
Project   Connect Sheffield

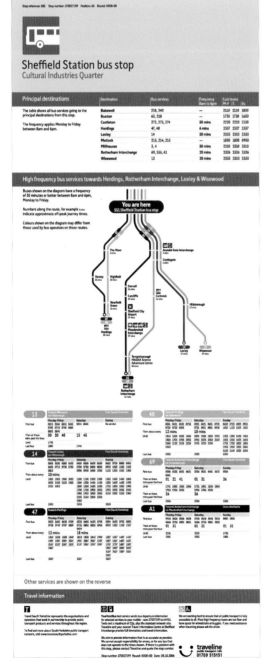

Sheffield City Council and its partners asked City ID to develop a concept and strategy for a range of products and services to help connect and reveal the City of Sheffield.

The Connect Sheffield concept puts the user at the centre of the design process ensuring that information is carefully planned to be relevant at each location. City ID developed the wayfinding strategy and worked closely with Atelier Works on the information and graphic identity for the pedestrian system, developing a set of identity elements that were inspired by the history of the city, including a unique typeface designed by Jeremy Tankard. The mapping system, produced with Endpoint, is simplified to promote pedestrian friendly routes and spaces, and is combined with Phil Sayer's monotone photography to help orientate and direct people, as well as provide the means to reveal information about the historic sites and areas of Sheffield.

A bespoke range of products was designed by Pearson Lloyd, who intended for the information to be key, and for the physical product to be as simple and understated as possible. The team also developed the concept and visual identity for an extensive system of public transport shelters and information displays that integrate transport and walking information at bus and tram stops across the city. The system is now being extended across the region.

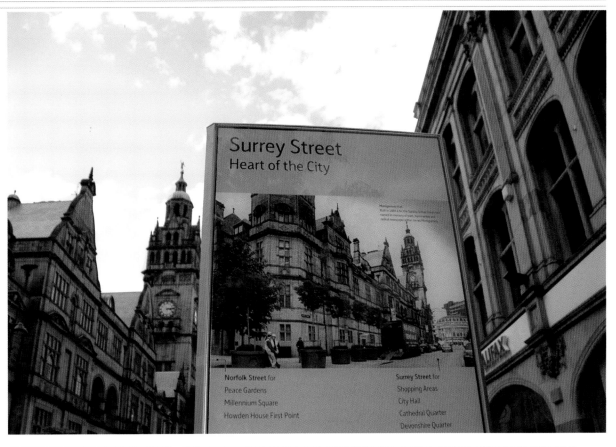

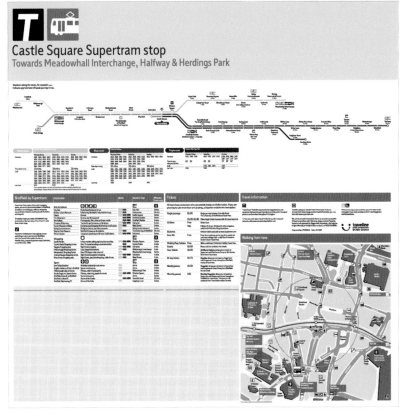

Design   Sans+Baum
Project   Future Map exhibition graphics

Future Map celebrates the best work of graduates from the London Institute, the umbrella body containing many of London's best-known art and design schools, and is held each year in the London Institute's gallery space near Bond Street. To emphasise the individual nature of the work, each student's contact details were printed on a series of 'jotter pads' throughout the exhibition. Sheets could be torn off and collected into a bag which was provided to visitors as they arrived. These bags were also sent out, shrink-wrapped, as private view invitations.

A series of essays on larger pads were also available for collection. There was no need for any graphics on the walls or a catalogue. The jotter pad dimensions acted as a module on which all of the exhibition design was based so that graphics and build became totally integrated.

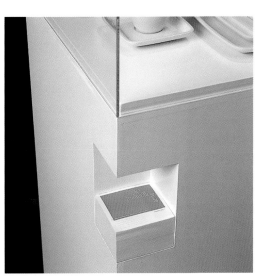

Design   Lust
Project   Open Ateliers 2000

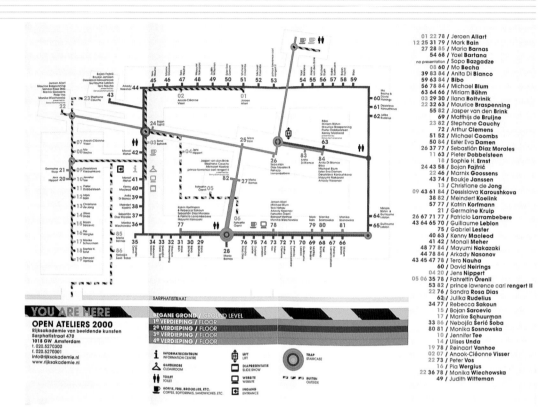

01 22 78 / Jeroen **Allart**
12 25 31 79 / Mark **Bain**
27 28 85 / Maria **Barnas**
54 68 / Yael **Bartana**
no presentation / Sopo **Bazgadze**
08 60 / Mo **Becha**
39 83 84 / Anita **Di Bianco**
59 63 84 / **Bibo**
56 78 84 / Michael **Blum**
63 64 66 / Miriam **Böhm**
03 29 30 / Ilana **Boltvinik**
22 32 63 / Maurice **Braspenning**
55 82 / Jasper **van den Brink**
69 / Matthijs **de Bruijne**
23 82 / Stephane **Cauchy**
72 / Arthur **Clemens**
51 52 / Michael **Coombs**
50 84 / Ester Eva **Damen**
26 33 77 / Sebastián **Díaz Morales**
11 63 / Pieter **Dobbelsteen**
18 / Sophie H. **Ernst**
24 43 58 / Bojan **Fajfrić**
22 46 / Marnix **Goossens**
43 74 / Christiane **de Jong**
09 43 61 84 / Dessislava **Karoushkova**
38 82 / Meindert **Koelink**
57 77 / Katrin **Korfmann**
21 / Germaine **Kruip**
26 67 71 77 / Patricio **Larrambebere**
43 64 65 70 / Guillaume **Leblon**
75 / Gabriel **Lester**
40 63 / Kenny **Macleod**
41 42 / Monali **Meher**
48 77 84 / Mayumi **Nakazaki**
44 78 84 / Arkady **Nasonov**
43 45 47 78 / Tero **Nauha**
60 / David **Neirings**
04 20 / Jens **Nippert**
05 06 35 78 / Fahrettin **Örenli**
53 82 / prince lawrence cari **rengert II**
22 76 / Sandra Rosa **Dias**
62 / Julika **Rudelius**
34 77 / Rebecca **Sakoun**
15 / Bojan **Sarcevic**
17 / Marike **Schuurman**
33 86 / Nebojša Šerić **Šoba**
80 81 / Monika **Sosnowska**
10 / Jennifer **Tee**
14 / Ulises **Unda**
19 78 / Reinaart **Vanhoe**
02 07 / Anook-Ciéonne **Visser**
22 73 / Peter **Vos**
16 / Pia **Wergius**
22 36 78 / Monika **Wiechowska**
49 / Judith **Witteman**

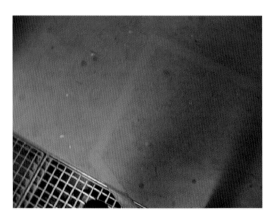

The Rijksakademie, Amsterdam, holds an event called
Open Ateliers when the public can visit the studios of
the artists attending the school. Because of the complex
nature of the building, a major complaint in previous years
was that no-one could find their way to all of the studios.
The decision to use a metro-like map with floor markings,
as used in institutions such as hospitals, led to the main
graphic element of the print work – floor-tape. A map
was therefore designed which led the public around the
building directly to the studio of choice: no-one got lost.

 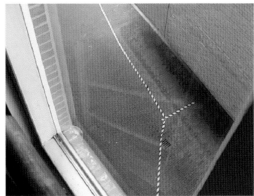 

Design	Frost Design
Project	Give & Take exhibition graphics

Faced with the task of producing graphics for an exhibition at the Victoria & Albert Museum (V&A) in London, Frost Design created a concept that embodied both a logo and a navigational system that ran through the entire space.

The exhibition juxtaposed permanent display artefacts with contemporary art, and the works were not confined to just one or two rooms, but ran throughout the entire museum. A strong navigational system to help guide the viewer through the labyrinth of exhibition rooms and corridors was therefore crucial. The designers' solution was to run a red stripe along the floors (a system frequently used in hospitals to guide patients to the appropriate ward). The red line also becomes a recurring motif, appearing in the exhibition logo and graphics, the 'V' of 'give' and the 'A' of 'take' becoming arrowheads.

Design	Lust
Project	Risk Perception carpet for InfoArcadia

InfoArcadia is an exhibition about data, information and the manner in which they are visualised. Information graphics, instruction manuals, information landscapes, data clusters are included, but so too are more personal ideas – like mapping one's life by marking events on food tin lids. The Dutch design company Lust was asked to make a piece which interpreted the data Paul Slovic gathered through surveys on people's perception of risks in 1988. Lust selected 81 'risks' from Slovic's collection of more than 40,000 answers. A way was needed to visualise the 'x-y matrix' on which the 'risks' were mapped.

The commissioner wanted a visualisation of three results of the research: factors such as 'controllable vs. uncontrollable' and 'known risk vs. unknown risk'; the desire of people for strict regulation of certain risks; and the importance of certain risks as signals to society. Lust decided that the visitor would form the third axis (z). The carpet measures $9^{27}/_{32}$ x $9^{27}/_{32}$ft (3 x 3 metres).

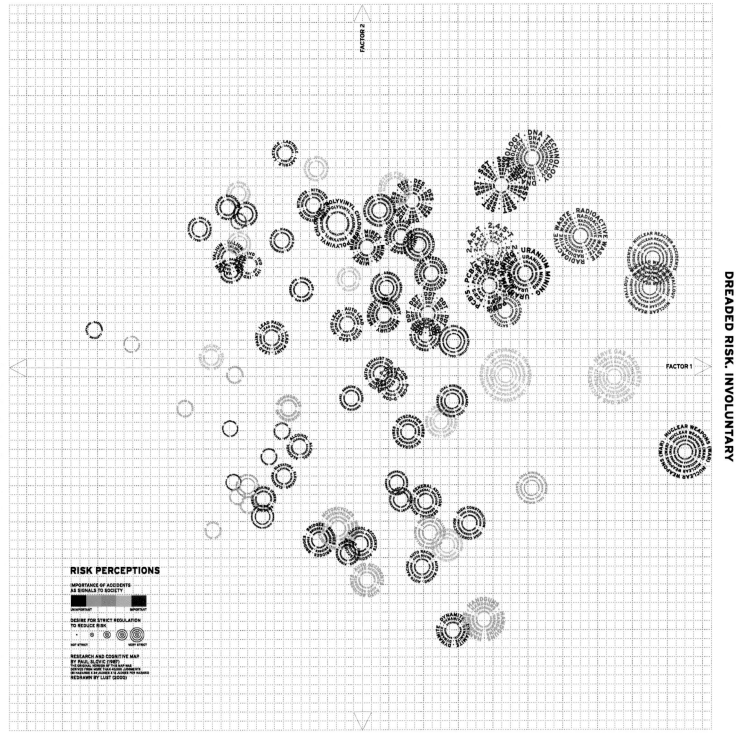

UNKNOWN RISK. NEW. DELAYED EFFECT

FACTOR 2

NOT DREADED RISK. VOLUNTARY

DREADED RISK. INVOLUNTARY

FACTOR 1

RISK PERCEPTIONS

IMPORTANCE OF ACCIDENTS
AS SIGNALS TO SOCIETY

UNIMPORTANT   IMPORTANT

DESIRE FOR STRICT REGULATION
TO REDUCE RISK

NOT STRICT   VERY STRICT

RESEARCH AND COGNITIVE MAP
BY PAUL SLOVIC (1987)
THE ORIGINAL VERSION OF THIS MAP WAS
DERIVED FROM MORE THAN 40,000 JUDGEMENTS
(81 HAZARDS X 34 JUDGES X 15 JUDGES PER HAZARD)
REDRAWN BY LUST (2000)

KNOWN RISK. OLD. IMMEDIATE EFFECT

Design   Peter Anderson
Project   Cayenne interior

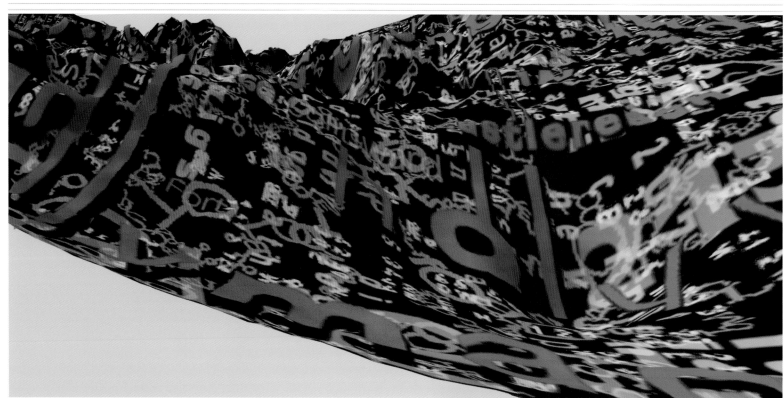

When Peter Anderson was commissioned to produce graphics for a stylish restaurant in Belfast, Northern Ireland called Cayenne, the resulting material became more art installation than just menu cover design. For a piece recessed into one wall of the restaurant (below), Anderson took as a starting point every surname in the Belfast telephone directory, then began to work this mass of typographic data into an abstraction of the Belfast street map. This random placement of names created some interesting instances of wordplay, and in a divided city where one can often tell the area where someone lives by their surname, the appearance of some names next to others created a talking point – or thinking point – for some more observant diners. Other elements of Anderson's design included a lenticular wall piece, mounted above the bar, called 'Mountain People' (left). Made up of map reference points for high points in the mountains around Belfast as well as grid references for cities around the world, the piece asks the question 'are mountain people curious? Do they always want to see what is on the other side?'

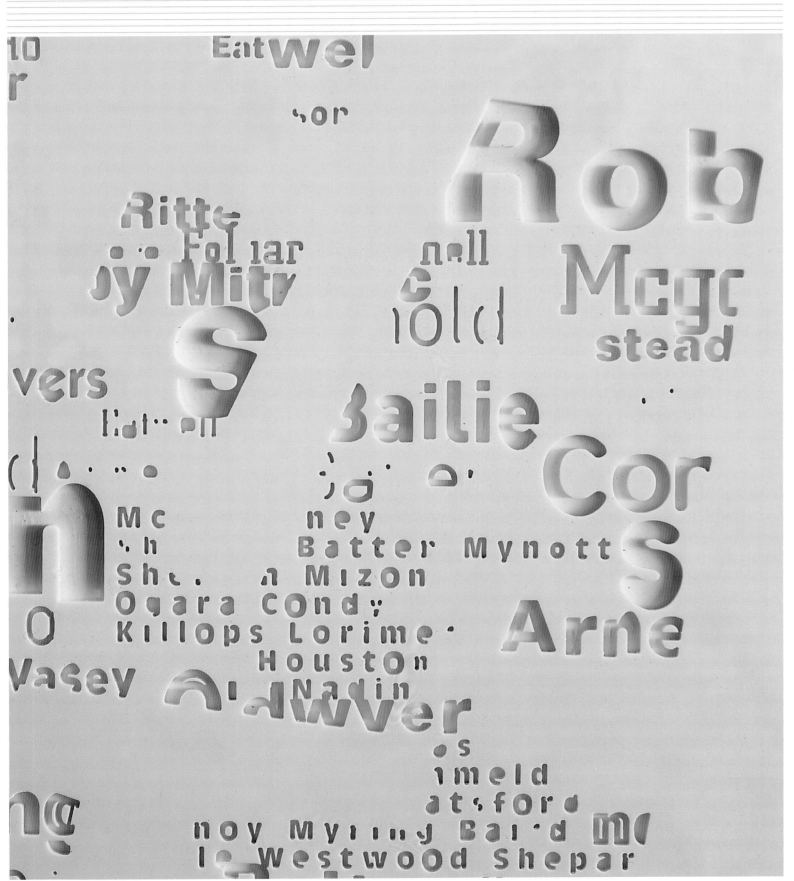

Design   Intégral Ruedi Baur et Associés
Project   Parc et Musée Archéologique de Kalkriese
Photography   Eva Kubinyi

This archeological museum is located at a site where the 'Germans' beat the Romans. It tries to retrace the battle using large iron plates installed in the ground on which inscriptions in Latin and German explain the course of events. Three pavilions, constructed from corrugated iron, connect this event to the contemporary world through the expression of sensations such as seeing, hearing and understanding. The large iron slabs work as both a pathway and a directional signage system, leading the visitor through the different parts of the museum. The typography on the slabs is raised and set in a bitmapped font, all in upper case, working as a counterbalance to the history of the museum. As the iron is untreated, the surface is gradually eroded by the elements, allowing the panels to work in harmony with the surrounding nature.

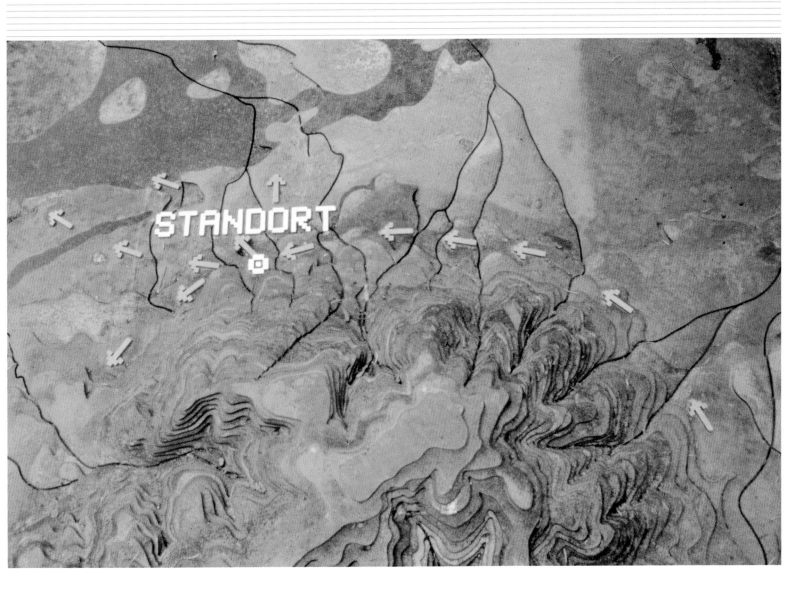

Design   Intégral Ruedi Baur et Associés
Project   Centre Pompidou, Paris
Photography   Blaise Adilon

The signage system developed by Ruedi Bauer for the Centre Georges Pompidou, Paris, is based on the idea of 'spatial explosion' of information usually contained in a single signage panel. Signage, in this case, equals scenography. Concentrations of words appearing in different languages express the interdisciplinarity and multi-culturalism present at the Centre Pompidou.

The signage system works on various surfaces and non-surfaces, including freely suspended neon typographic elements, and large format banners overprinted in numerous colours with the same word in various languages. The overall effect of the system is one of energy and immediacy. The interaction between surfaces and the open spaces all helps to build on the graphic intensity.

Design   Peter Anderson
Project   Poles of Influence

London-based graphic designer and artist Peter Anderson was commissioned to produce a work of art for the opening exhibition of the St. Lucia Museum of Contemporary Art, but on arriving on the Caribbean island, he discovered that the museum was not yet finished. This gave him some time to familiarise himself with the island and its culture. He discovered that tall, thin wooden poles were everywhere, their uses ranging from acting as props for banana trees and washing lines to building houses. As he was keen to produce a work of art that responded to its environment, he decided to use these wooden poles as an art installation which would extend across the entire island. He painted the sticks using a colour coding system and gave each stick a specific number, which ranged from his car registration number to an ex-girlfriend's phone number. These poles were then planted across the island in groups following a specific matrix, thereby creating a new set of co-ordinates for the island, and allowing islanders and tourists to weave their own stories around these strange interventions in the landscape.

Design   The Kitchen
Project   Ocean club signage system

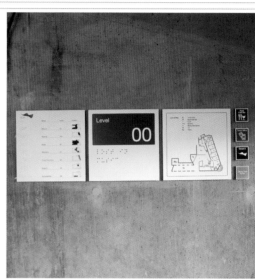

How do you create a navigation system for people who cannot see? That was the question facing graphic design consultancy The Kitchen when it was commissioned to create a signage system as part of its identity for Ocean. Ocean is one of the largest music venues in London with a capacity of 3000, and boasting three auditoriums over four levels.

The Kitchen attempted to devise a system that was as restrained as possible, working all the signs into a square format produced in enamelled metal panels. White backgrounds were applied to all the signs with a second colour chosen for each of the auditoriums.

All panels are split in half along a horizontal axis, with the text and icons shown in white out of the area colour at the top, braille text also reads across the foot of each panel. A further element of braille was applied to the sign, but this information was printed, not embossed, thereby becoming purely a surface effect, and adding a little humour to the otherwise austere signs (the text contains the titles of famous songs which are relevant to the area or information the sign depicts; the toilet sign reads 'Boys and Girls' by Blur, a sign showing the way upstairs reads 'Stairway to Heaven' by Led Zeppelin, and so on). This aspect of the signage has

proved to be successful among the partially sighted, who are able to read printed text as well as braille.

The system has proved to be highly successful, with a number of the panels being 'liberated' in the weeks after the new venue opened.

Design   City ID, MetaDesign London and PSD:Fitch
Project   Bristol Legible City

Welcome to Bristol

Bristol	H6	Camera Obscura	A3	Council House	H5	Maritime Heritage Centre	F7	St. Nicholas Markets	M4	Anchor Road	H6
Architecture Centre	K6	Central Library	H5	CREATE Centre	B7	Police Station	M3	Temple Meads Station	R6	Baldwin Street	K5
Arnolfini	K6	Christmas Steps	K4	Crown Court	K4	Red Lodge	H4	Tourist Information Centre	H6	Berkeley Place	F4
Bristol Cathedral	H5	City of Bristol College	G6	Explore@Bristol	H6	Register Office	N3	University of Bristol		Bond Street	P3
Bristol Hippodrome	K5	Clifton Suspension Bridge	A4	Galleries Shopping Centre	N3	RWA Art Gallery	F3	Students' Union	E3	Broadmead	N3
Bristol Industrial Museum	K7	Colston Hall	G5	Georgian House	G5	Shopmobility	N4	Victoria Rooms	F3	Broad Street	K4
Bristol Old Vic	M5	Commonwealth Museum	P6	IMAX Theatre@Bristol	K6	ss Great Britain	F6	Wills Memorial Building	G4	Clifton Down Road	C3
Bristol Zoo Gardens	B1	Corn Exchange	M4	John Wesley's Chapel	N3	St. George's Bristol	G4	Watershed	K5	Clifton Triangle	F3
Bus & Coach Station	M2			Magistrates' Court	K3	St. Mary Redcliffe	N7	Wildwalk@Bristol	K6	Corn Street	M4

Deanery Road	G5	Park Street	H4	Rupert Street	M3	The Horsefair	N2
High Street	M5	Penn Street	P3	St. Augustine's Parade	K5	The Mall	C4
King Street	K5	Prince Street	K6	St. James' Barton	N2	Trenchard Street	H4
Lewins Mead	K4	Queen Charlotte Street	K4	St. Paul's Road	F2	Union Street	M3
Marlborough Street	M2	Queen's Road	F3	Temple Gate	R7	Upper Maudlin Street	K2
Millennium Square	H6	Queen Square	M5	Temple Quay	R6	Victoria Street	N5
Narrow Quay	K6	Redcliffe Way	N6	Temple Way	P5	Welsh Back	M6
Nelson Street	M4	Regent Street	B5	The Centre Promenade	M6	Whiteladies Road	F2
Park Row	H4	Royal York Crescent	B5	The Grove	M6	Wine Street	M4

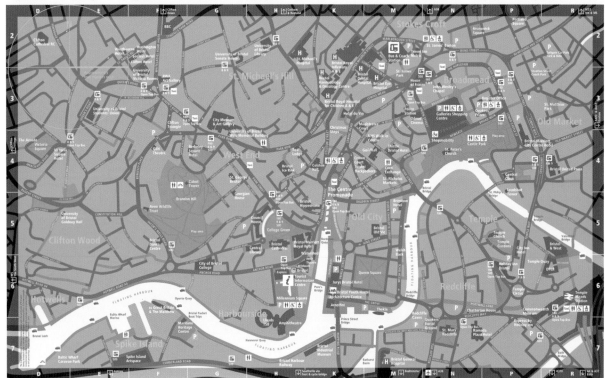

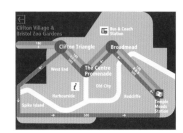

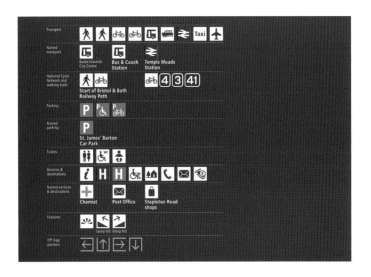

Bristol Legible City is a unique, award-winning project that aims to improve people's understanding and experience of the city through the implementation of identity, public realm, arts, information and transportation projects.

Bristol-based city legibility specialists City ID were commissioned by Bristol City Council to take the lead role in the concept, strategy development and design of the project, and have since been involved in the delivery of more than 40 projects working with a range of specialists that include information designers MetaDesign/AIG London, product designers PSD:Fitch/Lacock Gullam, cartographer and illustrator Russell Bell and manufacturers Wood & Wood.

Bristol Legible City includes a comprehensive city centre wayfinding system that connects points of arrival, key destinations, services and major city spaces. The system is designed to be intuitive and engaging. Following user testing, maps were used in a 'heads up' format to match the view of the user. They include a level of detail at a scale of 1:1000, including three-dimensional illustrations of buildings that help locate key attractions and services, as well as road crossings, steps and traffic-free zones to help users plan their route. Underpinning the planning was the idea that information should be well structured,

consistent and relevant. A print map was also designed to work as a companion to the system, which has now been extended into neighbourhood areas of the city.

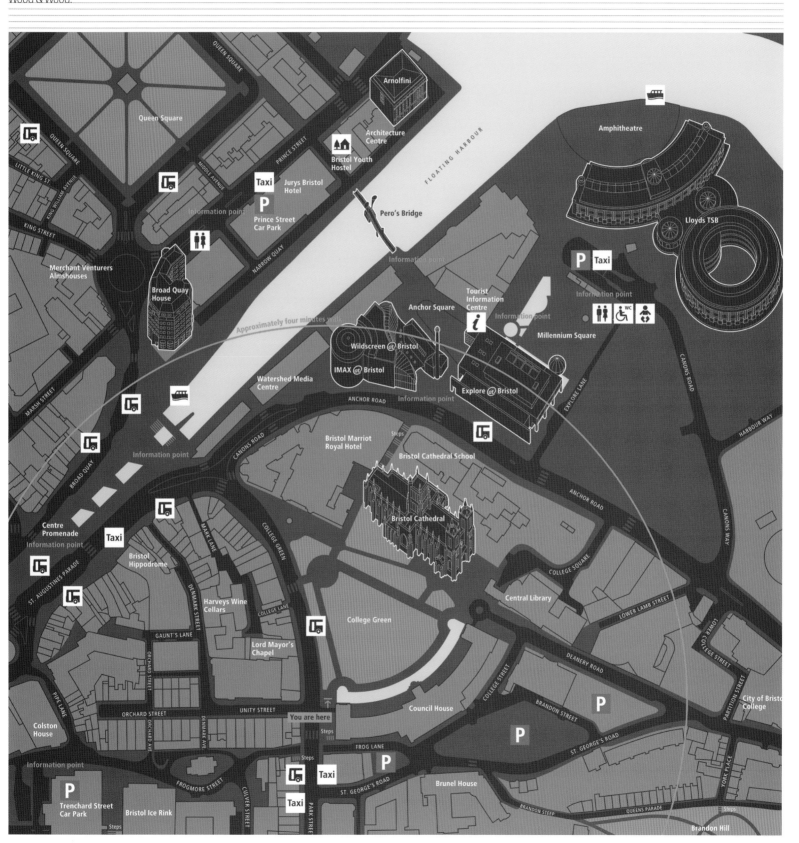

Design	Cartlidge Levene
Project	Selfridges Oxford Street (London) signage and wayfinding
Photography	Marcus Ginns

Department stores generate very noisy visual environments to work in, with numerous in-store concessions using a multitude of different graphic styles and tactics to shout for attention. London-based graphic design consultancy Cartlidge Levene was asked to devise a new navigational signage system for Selfridges on Oxford Street in London, one of the oldest and largest independent department stores in the city. The key aspect of the brief was to develop a flexible system that could be easily updated, allowing the store to regularly introduce new concessions and departments.

Cartlidge Levene worked with the product designer Julian Brown to develop a system of acrylic totems that encase the digitally-printed signage information. Newly updated informtion sheets can be easily installed within the acrylic frames by the in-store team. The large scale totems (up to 11^{31}/$_{64}$ft/3.5 metres high) are located at the escalators on each floor, forming a central information hub for the store.

The information totems are complemented by a series of hanging signage banners formed by two clear acrylic rods, which hold a digitally-printed information wrap. Again, this wrap can be easily updated as needed.

Design   Pentagram
Project   Bloomberg headquarters

Pentagram created signage, environmental graphics and media installations for the new corporate headquarters of Bloomberg, the financial news, data and analytics provider. The company occupies nine floors of a new 55-storey tower on Manhattan's East Side.

Wayfinding in the building is co-ordinated by number. Different floors are marked with translucent colour-coded resin numbers encased in glass, and a zipcode-like scheme is used for identifying different areas of each floor.

The sixth floor includes an area known as the 'Link', a three-storey glass bridge/winter garden that includes the main entrance to offices and communal terminals for staff and guests. Here, the designers created oversized news zippers that scroll on three sides of the space, including a media wall broken into four parallel bands that capture data from the Bloomberg live feeds. The flow of information complements the movement of people in the space, and the changing colours of the media wall transform the space throughout the day.

Design	Cartlidge Levene and Studio Myerscough	Design	Cartlidge Levene
Project	Barbican Centre signage and wayfinding	Map illustration	Russell Bell
Photography	Richard Learoyd and Tim Soar	Project	Barbican Centre printed map
		Photography	Sue O'Brien

Located in the heart of London, The Barbican Arts Centre has always proved to be a challenge to navigate. This signage and navigation system works in perfect harmony with the original 1960s concrete architecture. The system utilises a strong orange colour throughout, combined with a Futura Bold font set in lower case.

A key feature of the system is the use of super-scale numerals positioned by the side of the lifts. These floor-to-ceiling numbers are cut out from the orange facia to reveal the original rough concrete walls.

In addition to the signage system, a simple concertina folded map was produced to help new visitors navigate the centre. The map also uses the large-scale numbers on the back of the leaflet, which can be read through the paper onto the map side of the sheet. Again, the simple palette of orange and black/grey is used to good effect.

Design   Sans+Baum
Information design   Gail Mellows
Architects   DSDHA
Project   London Riverside's Employment Areas

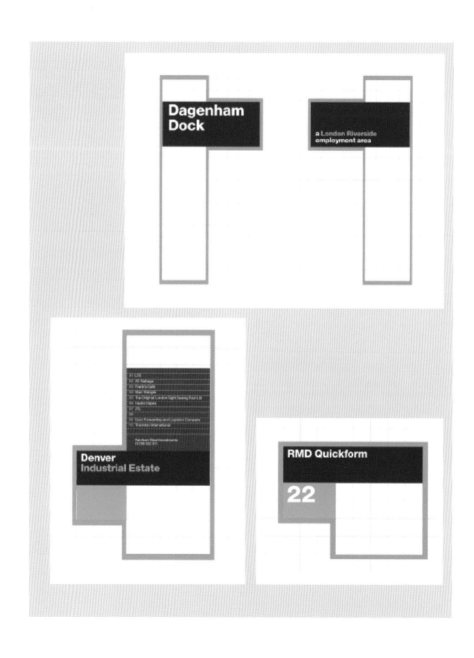

The design consultants Sans+Baum, in collaboration with wayfinder/information designer Gail Mellows and the architects DSDHA, created a road signage wayfinding system for London Riverside's Employment Areas, East London. The new system has helped to create and define unity in this large industrial area.

The signage system comprises a family of sign types: gateway signs, located on the roadside at entry points to the industrial areas; estate directories and single occupier signs, located at the entrance to an estate; and estate entrance signs, easily visible when approaching the entrance to an estate.

The system uses a palette of three shades of green, adding a natural colour scheme to an otherwise industrial landscape of concrete and metal.

Design   Base
Project   PASS – Scientific Adventure Park
Location   Belgium

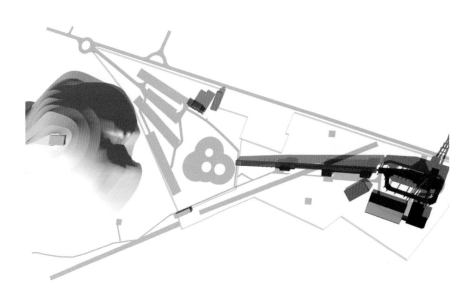

The graphic identity for this Scientific Adventure Park in Belgium was designed by Base, which was involved in every aspect of the graphic project from web site to building graphics. The interiors have the quality of a raw industrial plant, space station or bunker, and untreated structural materials such as concrete and steel are visible through the building. The signage and navigational system works directly with these raw materials: large panels are painted in bright colours, which relate to an on-screen virtual navigation map of the park. Large typography which is applied directly to the surface indicates zones or levels, while huge icons are applied to walls and floors marking lift shafts and ticket halls.

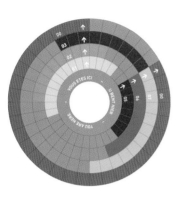
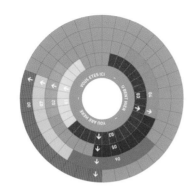
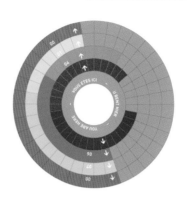
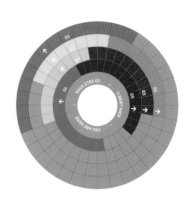

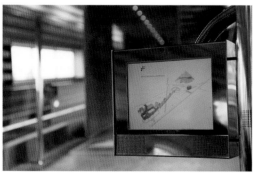

Design   Farrow Design
Project   Making the Modern World

Farrow Design was asked to design the permanent
exhibition 'Making the Modern World' at the Science
Museum in London.
At the entrance to the gallery is a
large black stone obelisk which contains a lightbox with
orientation graphics of the gallery. One of the most striking
features of the gallery is 'Carhenge', a stack of six cars
which extends right up to the roof. The plinth at the base
of this tower contains a flush-mounted graphic panel
housing information on each car. Smaller items are housed
in floor-standing boxes with back-lit panels on the top
plane showing information about the object and an LCD
monitor which shows footage of the object in action.

03 _ Information and space

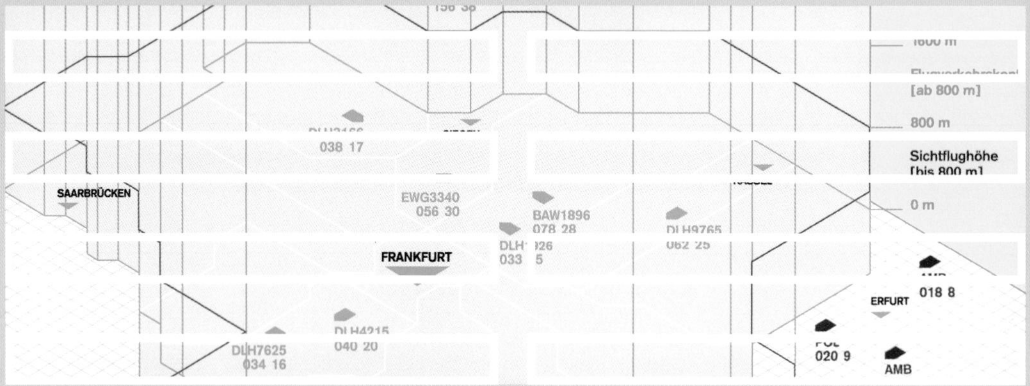

SAARBRÜCKEN

EWG3340
056 30

BAW1896
078 28

DLH9765
062 25

DLH 026
033 5

FRANKFURT

ERFURT   018 8

038 17

DLH7625
034 16

DLH4215
040 20

POL
020 9

AMB

1600 m

[ab 800 m]

800 m

Sichtflughöhe
[bis 800 m]

0 m

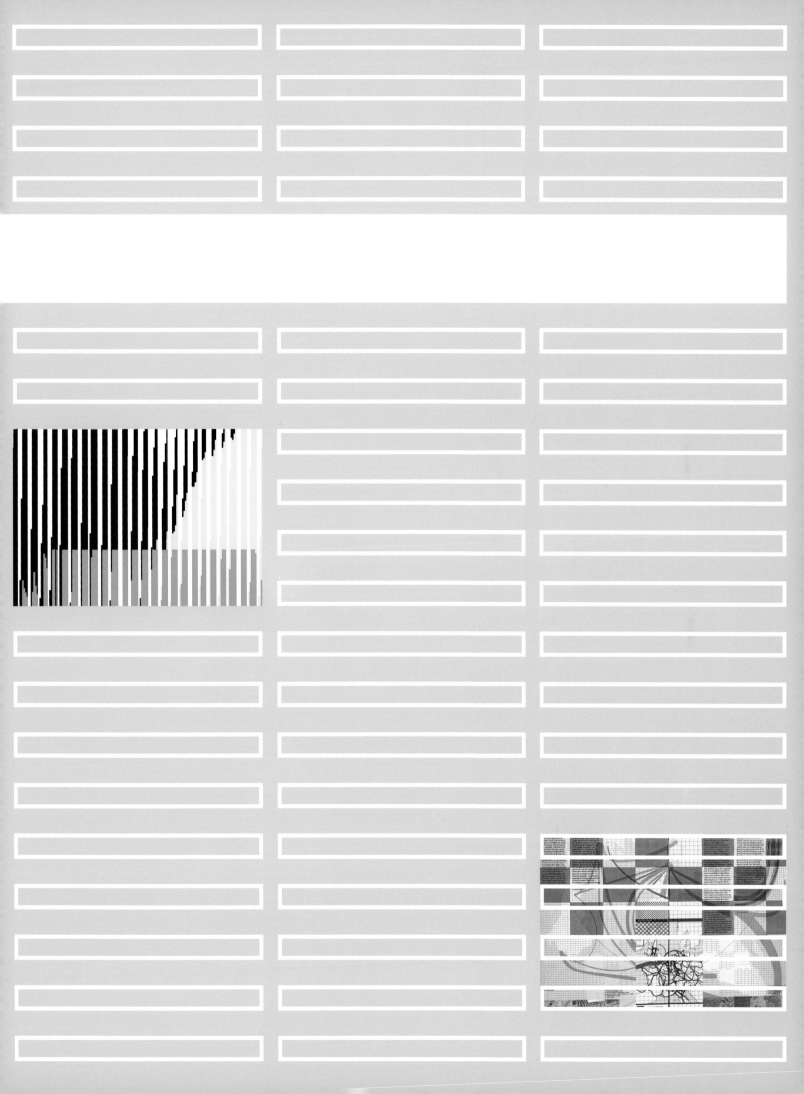

Information

Essay by William Owen
116/117

By teaching the simple facts of the shape, size and position of a country relative to all the others, the political map of the world has become intrinsic to our sense of national identity. When I was growing up, in Britain in the mid-1960s, our school maps portrayed the British Isles (we just called it 'England') sitting comfortably and naturally at the exact longitudinal centre of a flat world, north at the top and south at the bottom, the country subtly and significantly exaggerated in size by the Mercator projection and coloured prettily in pink. We learnt from the beginning that this was the natural way of things.

A lot of the rest of the world was pink, too: these were the twilight years of the British Empire. The map was probably 20 years old by then and its representation of demi-global dominion in superabundant pinkness had already been made obsolete by national liberation movements across Africa, the Mediterranean, Arabia, India, East Asia and the Caribbean. But it wasn't easy for a school geography department to keep up with the winds of change and so we clung to the fiction of empire.

The real use of this map, like most maps, was "to possess and to claim, to legitimate and to name" [1], in this case the assertion by the British state of sovereignty over itself and a large portion of the world, and the expression of the singular point of view that England lay at the centre of everything.

In the 35 years since I was at junior school ideas about possession and sovereignty have altered, possibly faster than maps have. The political map of the world has been redrawn, of course, with the creation within the former Soviet and Yugoslav Republics of nineteen new nation states and the destruction of one (the GDR). These are the kinds of absolute changes that conventional maps excel at: the transformation of political boundaries – lines on the ground - or of names, or of regimes. Rights were being reasserted in eastern Europe and Russia, but elsewhere national boundaries were becoming confused. The more interesting and subtle changes – for society and for cartography – have been those arising out of the integration of world trade, communications, politics, culture and population, and the diminishing importance of national political boundaries.

The inexorable progress of globalisation is a challenge to mapmakers. How do we define, in cartographic terms, contemporary political relations, or ideas about nearness and remoteness, relative size and wealth in a world where political alignment is multi-layered and distance is measured in air miles and bits per second? Harder still, how do we represent within a figurative geographical construct what it is to be British, Japanese, Nigerian or Turkish and how each nation fits within the world, when we each live, either in a literal or metaphorical sense, everywhere?

The inadequacy of the one-dimensional identity and the singular point of view described by a national boundary (and national colour, flag, anthem, bird…) should be self-evident, although like a school geography department we cling to old truths. Western topographical conventions are fixated on physical space, not just for the needs of navigation but also because they are rooted in asserting property relations – rights of ownership – and therefore the accurate description and allocation of territories (private or state) is paramount. Space, however, is increasingly distorted by the wealth or continuity of communications or by cultural influence and integration (who needs to be in California when Starbucks is round every corner?). Also, the assertion of absolute rights of ownership has relatively less meaning than access to goods and services (or to certain rights and privileges that in the modern world supersede citizenship: those accruing from educational qualifications, wealth or trading block membership). The possession of physical space and the representation of 'real' physical distance (and even navigation across it) has relatively less meaning than newer, more complex equations of proximity or privilege.

How do we define, in cartographic terms, ideas about nearness and remoteness, relative size and wealth in a world where distance is measured in air miles and bits per second?

Lust
Fietstocht door
Vinex-locaties
Den Haag
120/121

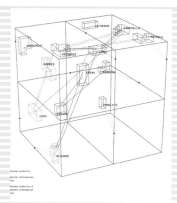

Lust
i³ map
128/129

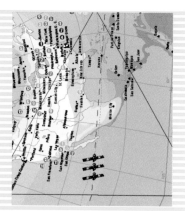

Damian Jaques
The MetaMap
136/137

Take Britain as an example of a vague, ambiguous and unresolved political state. There is a ghostly fragment of Empire in the Commonwealth and in dominion over Northern Ireland and diminutive offshore redoubts like the Turks and Caicos islands. There is a degree of internal fragmentation expressed in its one 'parliament' – British – and three 'assemblies' – Scottish, Welsh and Northern Irish. Britain's principal legal and economic policies are subject to those of the European Union, of which it is a leading member. However Britain remains outside the common currency Eurozone, and is semi-detached from the Schengen Agreement that defines border controls and police cooperation within the EU, dictating the all-important policy of who to let in and who to shut out. Other aspects of national sovereignty are influenced by membership of bodies such as Nato (defence policy) and the World Trade Organisation, (which defines tight parameters within which the economic and trade policies of its member states can flex).

Now take into account Britain's eclectic ethnic, cultural or linguistic traditions, or its central position within the global networked sub-economy in which a substantial minority of its citizens participate, in highly mobile supranational industries such as finance, media, software, oil and professional consulting. In the light of these multiple layers (and multiple maps?) what constitutes 'Britain' and 'Britishness' evidently still matters but has lost its old crispness.

Remapping a world in which global and national space/time co-exist requires a radical new approach, that allows topographical and topological representations to co-exist. Showing the 'true' proximity of one place to another in a jet-turbined, video-conferenced and Internet-enabled world requires a similarly multi-dimensional understanding of space and time, logical and physical. For example, if we measured distance by the duration, availability and price of air travel between two locations, rather than miles or kilometres, London would be very much 'nearer' to New York than to, say, Athens; or we could measure connectivity not by roads, railways or shipping lanes – as my mid-1960s atlas did – but by the number of Internet users and ISPs, or the price of voice telephony, the number of mobile users per population, the connection speed and miles of optical fibre, the number of television stations.

Such a map of proximity and connectivity would reveal a chain of massively connected global cities girdling the earth: in Europe – London, Paris and Frankfurt; in the Middle East – Dubai; in the Far East – Kuala Lumpur, Singapore, Hong Kong, Shanghai, Tokyo, Sydney; in the Americas – Sao Paolo, San Francisco, New York. Huge swathes of the world – predominantly but not exclusively in Africa and Asia – would be seen to be almost entirely disconnected from this hyper-concentration of activities and resources.

"The new networked sub-economy of the global city occupies a strategic geography that is partly deterritorialised, cuts across borders, and connects a variety of points on the globe. It occupies only a fraction of its local setting, its boundaries are not those of the city where it is partly located, nor those of the 'neighbourhood'."[2]

Where are the boundaries located, in a world in which the power of a non-government organisation (say Greenpeace), a media network (CNN) and a global corporation (Shell) are as significant in shaping environmental policy as a national government?

The boundaries lie in multiple dimensions, and not merely along national borders. They cross the routes of cross-border migration and encircle linguistic concentrations; they plot the activities of global corporations and their influence on our food, entertainment and health; they pinpoint the hotspots of international crime; they lie around trade zones and regions (or philosophies) of political alignment; they follow the contour lines of equal wealth, education, skills or connectivity; they are intersected and overlaid by specialised human activities (such as finance or media) or key nodal points of physical or digital exchange (Heathrow Airport, Wall Street, Dubai Internet City, the golf course at Palm Springs).

Our sense of place and position, and our understanding of the relations between things, their dimensions and attributes (true or false), is forged and reinforced by their representation on the map. By making these new facts visible, and revealing the coincidence of logical and physical objects or the rapid oscillation and contradiction between global and local points of view, then we should have a better map.

[1] Denis Wood, ibid.

[2] 'Obbis Terrarum, Ways of Worldmaking, cartography and Contemporary Art', ed. King and Brayer, Ludion Press, Ghent/ Amsterdam 2000

Design   Lust
Project   'Stad in Vorm'

INHOUDSOPGAVE

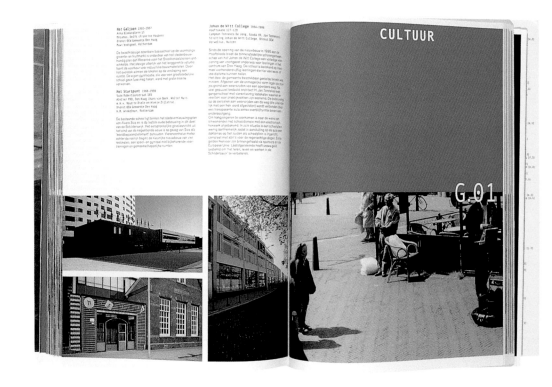

CULTUUR

G.01

This book, documenting the architectural projects found in The Hague, was designed by Dutch design consultancy Lust. The photography, by Guus Rijven, is careful to show not only the facades and spaces of the buildings, but also the architecture in context – peopled by those who live and work in the buildings.

The design of the book is based on a classification system which helps to guide the reader through several layers of information throughout the book. The ten chapters, each covering a different genre of architectural planning, are represented by specific colours. These colours are combined with an alphabetic 'numbering' system, which runs from A to J. Therefore, each building is given a distinctive 'serial number' comprised of the section letter and colour. On the inside of the dust jacket, several maps of The Hague are presented, showing only the areas mentioned in the text. Thus a cluster of green numbers on the map reveals, in an intuitive way, that that part of the city is mainly residential.

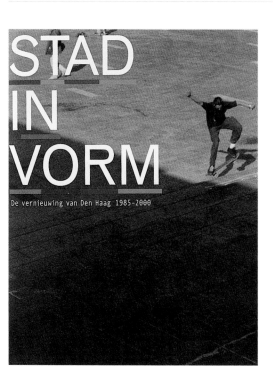

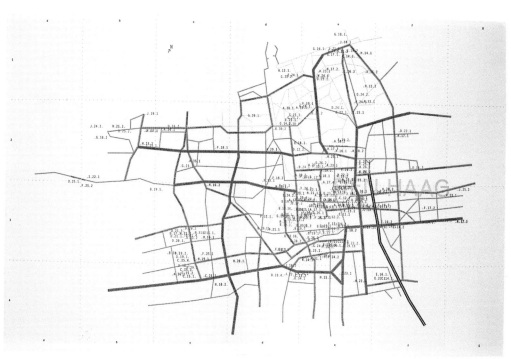

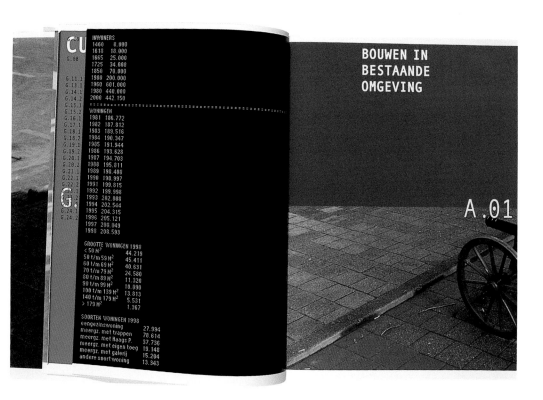

Design   Lust
Project   Fietstocht door Vinex-locaties Den Haag

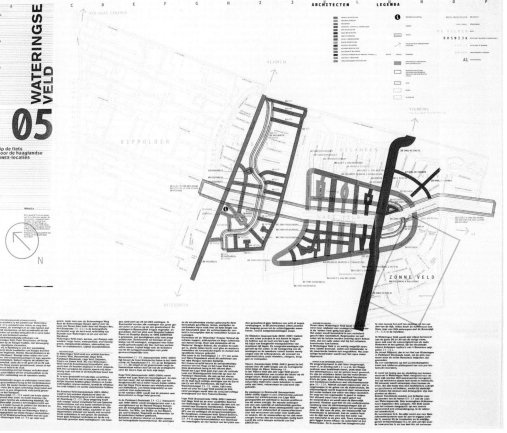

In celebration of Architecture Day in Holland, a set of maps were published to describe cycling tours of the special architectural projects built in the 'vinex' communities of The Hague (public lands set aside by the government of the Netherlands for suburban growth). A matrix was designed as an index to help users quickly find either the streets where projects are located, or the architects who built them. The street names form the y-axis and the architects' names form the x-axis. Each architect is given a colour, thereby making it simple to spot an architect and their projects on the map. The colour scheme of the matrix is defined by the alphabetical order of the street names, which gives the matrix of each map a unique 'colour fingerprint'. The 'fingerprint' of each matrix is then used as the cover panel for its respective map. All three fingerprints stacked on top of each other then form the cover for the whole piece.

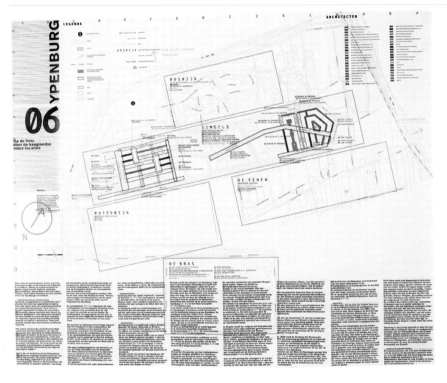

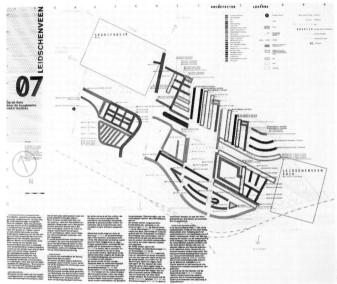

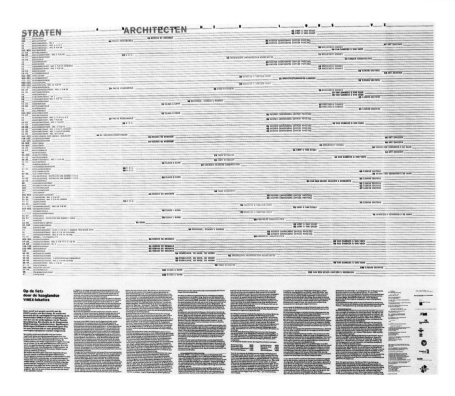

Design   Bibliothéque
Project   InterSections

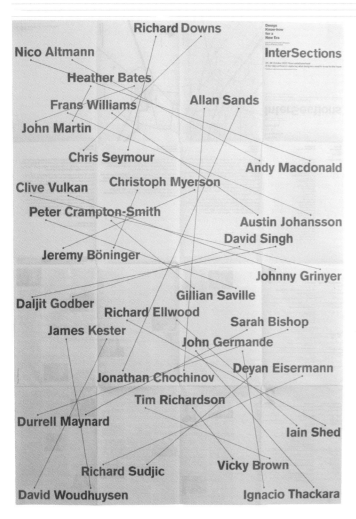

The theme of the 2007 InterSection conference was to explore what designers need to know for the future. The conference featured over 30 speakers from the worlds of product design, graphics, new media, industrial design, education and the media, and the conference was keen to promote lively debate between these key speakers.

The accompanying A5 (5⅘ x 8³⁄₁₀in) leaflet, which unfolds to a large A1 (23²⁄₅ x 33¹⁄₁₀in) poster printed in green, blue and black on thin Bible paper, clearly conveys the 'interaction' message of the conference. On the poster side, the first and last names of the key speakers in the conference are mixed up - Peter Saville and Gillian Crampton-Smith become Peter Crampton-Smith and Gillian Saville. To highlight this, the mixed-up names are displayed in green and blue with a network of connecting lines, allowing the reader to navigate back to the correct first and last name. The poster acts as a map, showing potential routes of interaction that may take place during the event between different individuals.

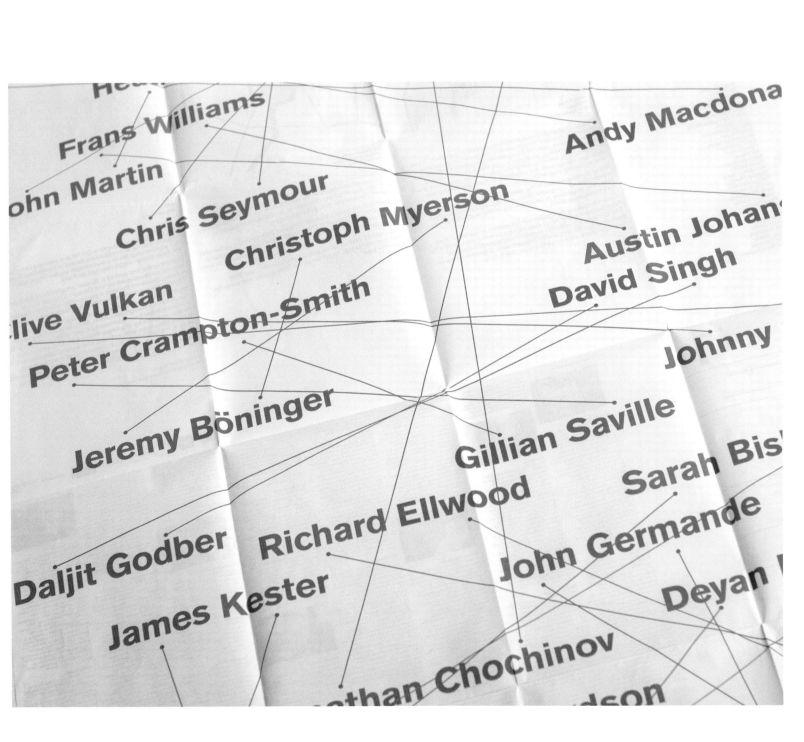

Design   Sandra Niedersberg
Project   London Connections –
            Who got to know whom where when and how?

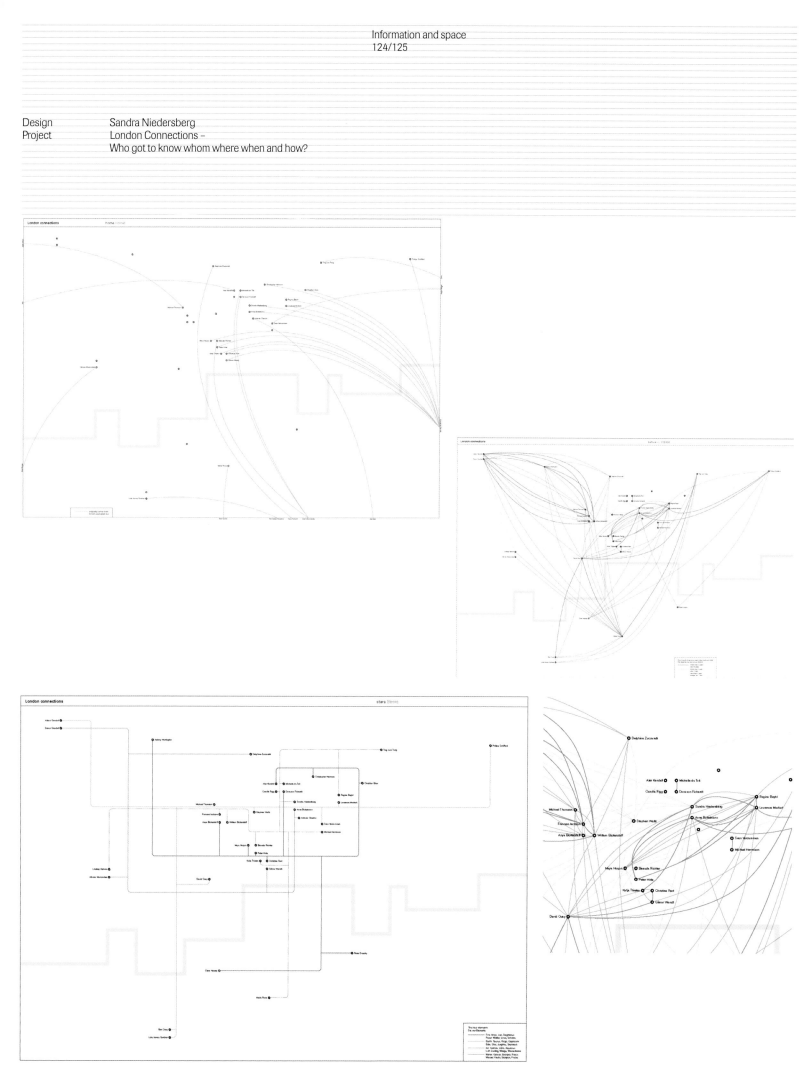

The 'six degrees of separation' theory claims that any two people are connected to each other through a maximum of six friends or associates – assuming that everyone knows a hundred people and those hundred people each know another hundred. In this way six connections are enough for the six billion people living on the earth.

Using this information as an inspiration, Sandra Niedersberg mapped and analysed the way she made friends and acquaintances over a five-month period after moving from Germany to London. The research was extended to include interviews with each contact which formed a book. With the information amassed she also created a series of A2 (16½ x 23⅗in)

maps printed onto translucent paper allowing the different levels to be over-laid to show further associations.

Each map uses the geography of London as its framework, reduced to a symbolic representation of the river Thames. Each person is represented by a dot and their name, the position of which corresponds to where they live. All the co-ordinate dots appear on every map, but a person's name only appears if they have a connection on that particular map. Each map shows different statistics for different situations, such as living, home, work, institutions, school, meeting points and so on, with colour coding used to reveal further levels of information.

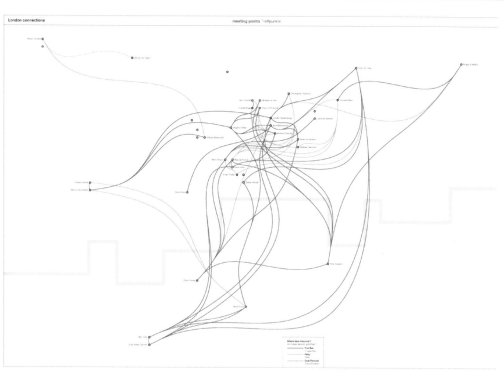

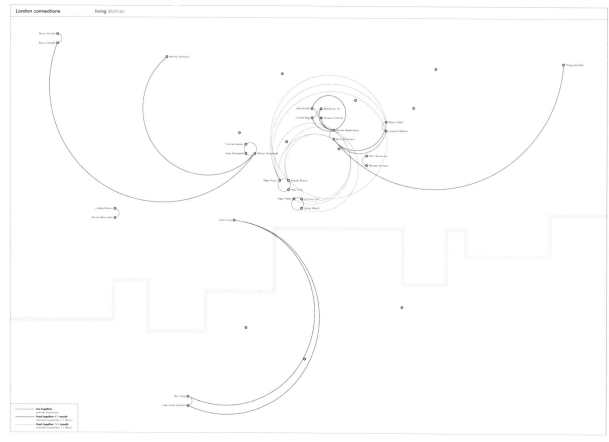

Design   Joost Grootens
Project   Metropolitan World Atlas

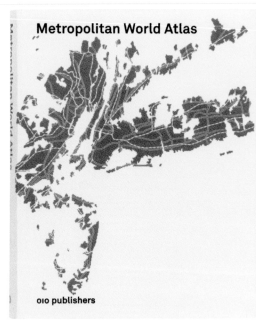

Metropolitan World Atlas

oıo publishers

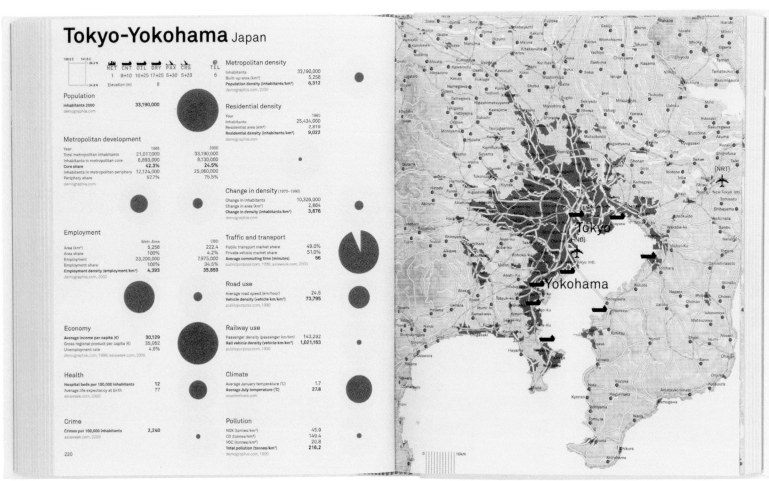

Tokyo-Yokohama Japan

MET	CNT	OIL	DRY	PAX	CRG		@ TEL
1	9+10	10+25	17+25	5+30	5+23		6
	Elevation (m)				8		

Metropolitan density
Inhabitants	33,190,000
Built-up area (km²)	5,258
Population density (inhabitants/km²)	**6,312**
demographia.com, 2000	

Population
Inhabitants 2000	**33,190,000**
demographia.com	

Residential density
Year	1985
Inhabitants	25,434,000
Residential area (km²)	2,819
Residential density (inhabitants/km²)	**9,022**
demographia.com	

Metropolitan development
Year	1965	2000
Total metropolitan inhabitants	21,017,000	33,190,000
Inhabitants in metropolitan core	8,893,000	8,130,000
Core share	42.3%	24.5%
Inhabitants in metropolitan periphery	12,124,000	25,060,000
Periphery share	57.7%	75.5%
demographia.com		

Change in density (1970-1990)
Change in inhabitants	10,326,000
Change in area (km²)	2,664
Change in density (inhabitants/km²)	**3,876**
demographia.com	

Employment
	Metr. Area	CBD
Area (km²)	5,258	222.4
Area share	100%	4.2%
Employment	23,200,000	7,975,000
Employment share	100%	34.5%
Employment density (employment/km²)	**4,393**	**35,859**
demographia.com, 2000		

Traffic and transport
Public transport market share	49.0%
Private vehicle market share	51.0%
Average commuting time (minutes)	**56**
publicpurpose.com, 1990; asiaweek.com, 2000	

Road use
Average road speed (km/hour)	24.5
Vehicle density (vehicle km/km²)	**73,795**
publicpurpose.com, 1990	

Economy
Average income per capita (€)	**30,129**
Gross regional product per capita (€)	35,052
Unemployment rate	4.6%
demographia.com, 1996; asiaweek.com, 2000	

Railway use
Passenger density (passenger km/km)	143,292
Rail vehicle density (vehicle km/km²)	**1,021,163**
publicpurpose.com, 1990	

Health
Hospital beds per 100,000 inhabitants	**12**
Average life expectancy at birth	77
asiaweek.com, 2000	

Climate
Average January temperature (℃)	1.7
Average July temperature (℃)	**27.8**
weatherbase.com	

Crime
Crimes per 100,000 inhabitants	**2,240**
asiaweek.com, 2000	

Pollution
NOX (tonnes/km²)	45.9
CO (tonnes/km²)	149.4
VOC (tonnes/km²)	20.8
Total pollution (tonnes/km²)	**216.2**
demographia.com, 1990	

220

0   10km

The Metropolitan World Atlas documents a total of 101
metropolises and analyses them through a combination
of same-scale ground plans and statistics, with categories
ranging from population density and data traffic to air pollution.
In order for readers to understand the
information intuitively, a system of orange dots was
introduced, varying in size to represent visually how a given
city compares to others in any category. World data maps
of these statistics offer additional visual comparisons.
The book is printed in five colours, including metallic
blue and Day-Glo orange, with a tinted varnish.

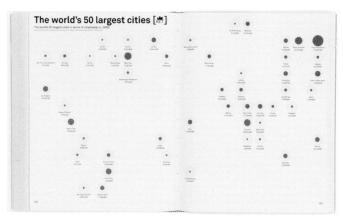

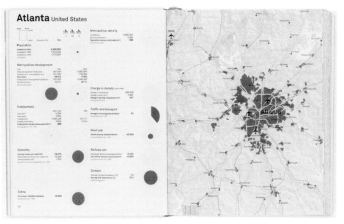

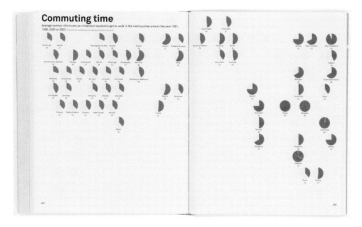

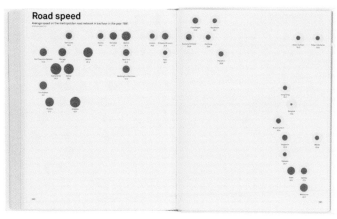

Design   Lust
Project   I³ Map

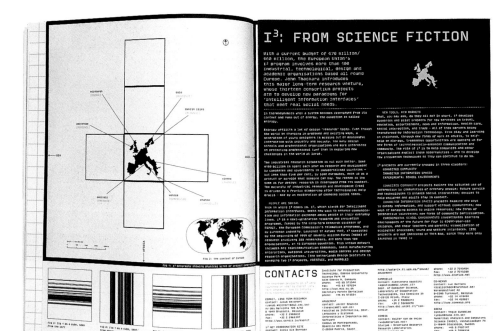

I³: FROM SCIENCE FICTION

With a current budget of €70 million/
$60 million, the European Union's
I³ program involves more than 100
industrial, technological, design and
academic organisations based all round
Europe. John Thackara introduces
this major long-term research venture,
whose thirteen consortium projects
aim to develop new paradigms for
'intelligent information interfaces'
that meet real social needs.

In thermodynamics when a system becomes disengaged from its context and runs out of energy, the condition is called entropy.

Entropy afflicts a lot of design 'research' today. Even though the world is changing in profound and exciting ways, a generation of young designers is missing out on meaningful interaction with industry and society. Too many design schools and professional organisations are more interested in protecting professional turf than in exploring new challenges in the world at large.

The industrial research situation is not much better. Some €100 billion is spent each year on research and development by companies and governments in industrialised countries — but less than five per cent, by some estimates, ends up as a product or service that someone can buy. The reason is the same as for design: research is disengaged from its context. The majority of industrial research and development (R&D) is driven by a frantic scavenging after technological Holy Grails — not by an exploration of changing social needs.

PEOPLE ARE SOCIAL

This is where I³ comes in. I³, which stands for Intelligent Information Interfaces, seeks new ways to enhance communication and information exchange among people in their everyday lives. I³ is a next-generation research and innovation programme, funded by the long-term research division of ESPRIT, the European Commission's Telematics programme, and by European industry. Launched in Autumn 1997, I³ consisted by the beginning of 1999 of seventy million Euros (ecus) of research involving 300 researchers, and more than 100 organisations, in 15 European countries. This unique network includes R&D telecommunication companies, small manufacturing enterprises, national universities, media centres and design research organisations. (The Netherlands Design Institute is managing two I³ projects, PRESENCE, and MANPOLE)

NEW TOOLS, NEW MARKETS

What, you may ask, do they all do? In short, I³ develops scenarios and pilot projects for new services in travel, education, entertainment, news and information, health care, social interaction, and trade — all of them markets being transformed by information technology. From play and learning in childhood, through new forms of work as adults, to self-help in old-age, tremendous opportunities are opening up for new forms of technologically-enhanced communication and community. The role of I³ is to help companies and other organisations exploit these opportunities — and to develop new innovation techniques so they can continue to do so.

I³ projects are currently grouped in three clusters:
CONNECTED COMMUNITY
INHABITED INFORMATION SPACES
EXPERIMENTAL SCHOOL ENVIRONMENTS

CONNECTED COMMUNITY projects explore the situated use of information by communities of ordinary people; future service and technologies to enhance social interaction; devices to help children and adults stay in contact.

INHABITED INFORMATION SPACES projects examine new ways to embody information, and support virtual communities; new ways of managing access to online resources; new forms of interactive television; new forms of community participation.

EXPERIMENTAL SCHOOL ENVIRONMENTS investigates learning environments of the future for four to eight-year-old children, and their teachers and parents; visualisation of ecological processes; sound and gesture interfaces. (ESE projects are not indicated on this map, since they were only launched in 1998) >>

CONTACTS

Institute for Production
Technology, Odense University
Science Park 10
5230 Odense M, Denmark
phone: +45 65 573946
fax: +45 63 157224
http://www.mip.ou.dk
secretary Marete Bertelsen
phone: +45 65 573551

The thirteen projects in I³ were launched in 1997 by ESPRIT Life Long Learning / Work programme — the EU programme's long-term research division.

ESPRIT, LONG TERM RESEARCH
contact: Jakob Weirbert
i.weiub.etr@cortell.cec.be)
Av des Nerviens 105 6/42
B-1049 Brussels, Belgium
phone: +32 2 2960632
fax: +32 2 2961327
http://www.cordis.lu/esprit

I³ NET COORDINATION SITE
contact: Niklas Eik Borhaus
cnweb@dai.bu.dk)
The Maersk Mc-Kinney Moller

APUSEMENT
contact: Javier Seputola
(fseputola@fi.upm.es)
Facultad de Informatica, Dept.
Lenguajes y Sistemas
Informaticos e Ingenieria del
Software
Campus de Montegancedo,
Boadilla del Monte
E-28660 Madrid, Spain
phone: +34 91 3367402
fax: +34 91 3367412

http://asterix.fi.upm.es/~amuse/
amusement

CAMPIELLO
contact: Alessandra Agostini
(agostini@dsi.unimi.it)
Dept. of Computer Science,
Laboratory of Cooperation
Technologies, Via Comelico 39
I-20135 Milan, Italy
phone: +39 2 55006313
fax: +39 2 55006276
http://www.dsi.unimi.it/~campiello

COMRIS
contact: Walter van de Velde
(wvdv@starlab.net)
Starlab - Riverland Research
Research Laboratories
Excelsiorlaan 42
B-1930 Zaventem, Belgium

phone: +32 2 7215494
fax: +32 2 7215380
http://www.starlab.net

CO-NEXUS
contact: Luc Mertens
(bibliotheek@turnhout.be)
Warandestraat 42
B-2300 Turnhout, Belgium
phone: +32 14 419494
fax: +32 14 420821
http://www.comexus.org

ERENA
contact: Yngve Sundblad
(yngve@nada.kth.se)
Numerical Analysis and Computing
Science (NADA), Valhallavägen 79
S-10044 Stockholm, Sweden
phone: +46 8 7907667
fax: +46 8 7908930
http://www.nada.kth.se/erena

I³ is a design programme of the European Union involved in research into intelligent information interfaces. As a contribution to the design publication IF/THEN, design company Lust designed a map which showed the relationships between the projects of the 71 institutions involved with I3. It was important to show which project was associated with which other project, whether geographically or conceptually. To map the spatial relationships between the institutions, a cube representing the world was used which was then deconstructed to reveal the existing and virtual connections of the corresponding projects. The map, although certainly informative in nature, also reveals the 'virtual' or 'experimental' aspect of each project. As well as hinting at the name of the programme, the choice of the cube was also a conceptual necessity since it afforded multiple geometries in which to visualise the connections. This map was designed by Lust for the Werkplaats Typografie, Arnhem, Holland.

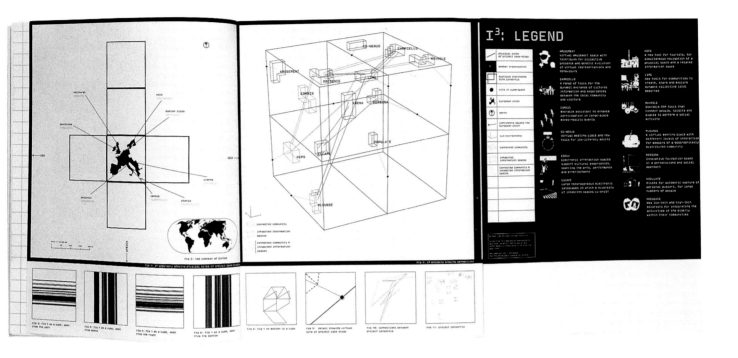

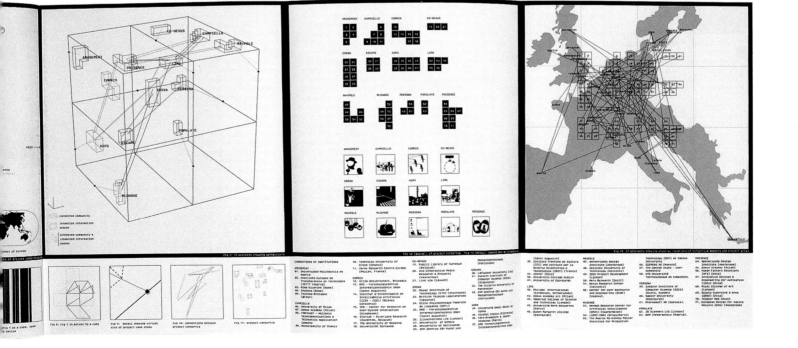

Design   Nick Bell Design
Project   'Lost and Found' exhibit

Nick Bell was invited by the British Council to create a piece of work for an exhibition in Belgium, titled 'Lost and Found'. He designed a map in the form of a tablecloth which uses typography to show the wettest and driest parts of England and Wales, and simultaneously explores the influence of invaders and immigrants on the language. Screenprinted onto paper damask banqueting roll is a list of nearly all the rivers that drain off Britain to the north, south, east and west. When the work was exhibited, pots of crayons were placed on the tablecloths (covering tables in the gallery refrectory), inviting vistors to comment on what they had seen. The list of French, Celtic, Norse,

Roman, Flemish and Dutch river names all found in England and Wales are testament to a rich and varied history. The map, the designer suggests, makes the point that, "despite being an island race, with an occasionally isolationist stance, the history of the country seems always to have been multi-cultural."

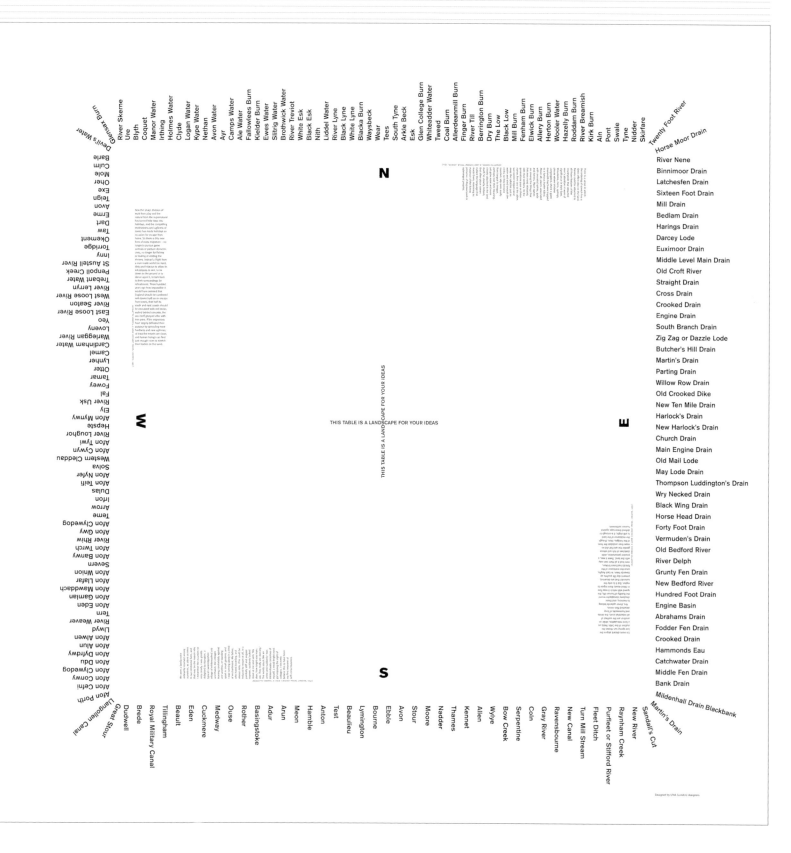

Design   Lust
Project   HotelOskarEchoKiloVictorAlphaNovemberHotelOscarLimaLimaAlphaNovemberDelta

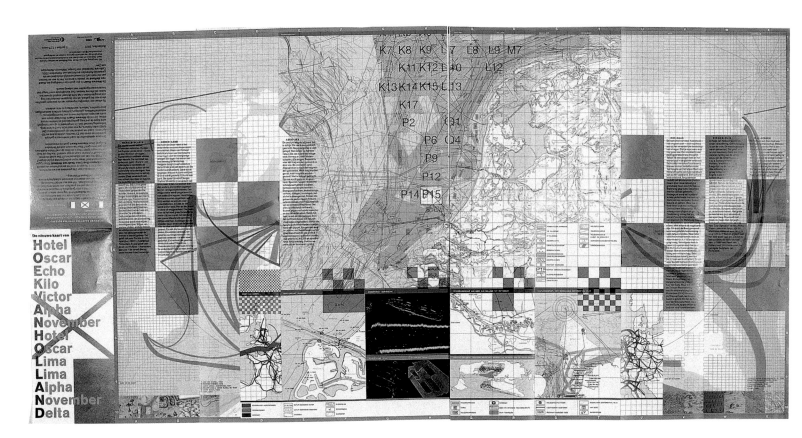

To highlight Hoek van Holland (Hook of Holland) as the 'beach & water recreation area' of Rotterdam during 2001, the year the city was European cultural capital, a map was published which revealed the many facets of Hoek van Holland: historical, economic, industrial, residential, maritime, recreational, and so on. A two-metre-long (6⁹⁄₁₆ft) sheet was needed to cover the broad range of information presented in the map. To keep the map convenient and easy to use despite its size, a useful folding system was devised that eliminated the trouble of having to continually fold and re-fold the map to see the necessary information. As a result, the map can actually be used as four maps, each giving a greater level of detail than the one that follows it: Hoek van Holland, the North Sea, Europe

and the world. Each folded variant shows information pertaining to that specific area, as well as showing the relation to the bigger area around it. A special projection of the world was also designed that placed Hoek van Holland in the middle of the map. On the other side of the map, the tidal and lunar information of Hoek van Holland is given for a complete year. Full moon is represented by a solid blue, while the new moon is represented by a ten per cent shading of the same blue. The stages of the moon in between are shown by increasing the percentage of blue. Seen as a whole, the function system symbolises the ebb and flow of the tides.

The map also records the position of site-specific art installations created for Hoek van Holland, providing another point of contact between the user of the map and the area.

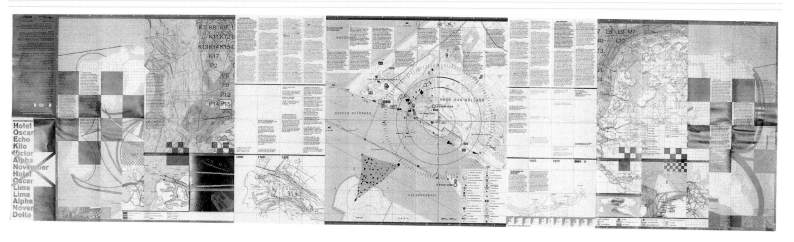

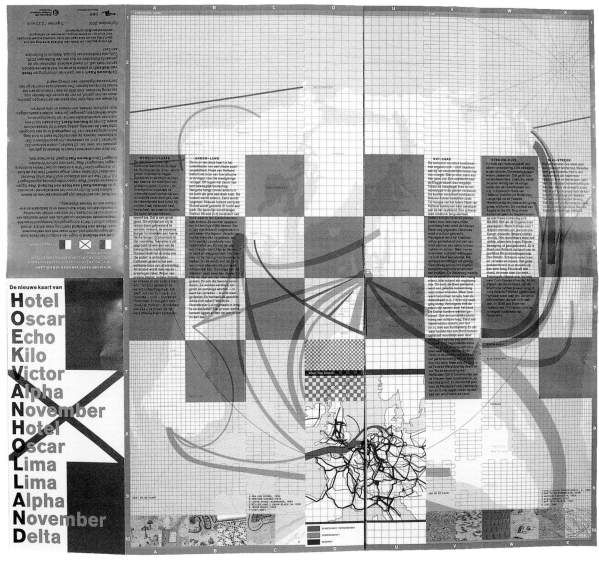

Design   Pentagram
Project   Global Cities

LONDON +6

ISTANBUL +17

LOS ANGELES +9

CAIRO +23

TOKYO +3

SHANGHAI +31

MEXICO CITY +25

MUMBAI +42

SAO PAULO +25

JOHANNESBURG +5

URBAN GROWTH: PEOPLE PER HOUR

340

20%

DENSITY

HALF OF EGYPT'S
70 MILLION
PEOPLE LIVE WITHIN A
100 KM
RADIUS OF CAIRO
(COMPARED WITH 12 MILLION PEOPLE WITHIN A 100KM RADIUS AROUND LONDON)

SOME OF
CAIRO'S
INFORMAL
BUILDINGS
REACH
14
STOREYS
HIGH

56%

CAIRO

This exhibition was developed from a show at the Venice Architecture Biennale in 2006 by the Tate curatorial team, in association with Professor Richard Burdett and his team at the London School of Economics (LSE), and with Pentagram providing art direction throughout.

Global Cities looks at five major issues – size, speed, form, density and diversity – and their effects on 10 major urban centres: Cairo, Istanbul, Johannesburg, London, Los Angeles, Mexico City, Mumbai, Sao Paulo, Shanghai and Tokyo. The exhibition places comparative socio-economic and geographic data alongside video and photography by 20 artists and architects and specially

commissioned London-inspired work by Nigel Coates, Zaha Hadid and Patrick Schumacher, Fritz Haeg, Rem Koolhaas, Nils Norman and Richard Wentworth.

Pentagram collaborated with academics from the LSE to produce the information graphics, which form the core of the ground floor of the exhibition, establishing an interchange between the LSE's city data and the work of artists and architects. Bold typographic statements complement clear information graphics and restrained graphic language communicates key facts that add context to the artwork.

Design   Damian Jaques
Project   The MetaMap

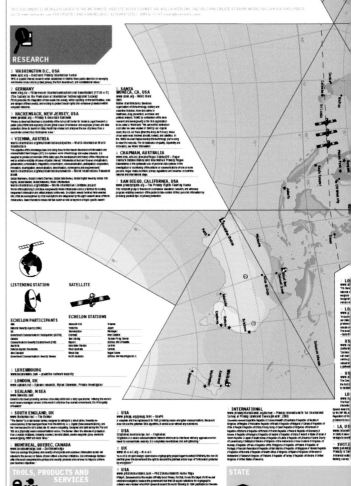

This large format map of the world uses the Fuller Projection – Dymaxion. Originally devised by the mathematician, designer and engineer Buckminster Fuller, this system allows the map to be cut-out and folded to form a three-dimensional globe. The MetaMap was developed by Mute magazine and is concerned with global surveillance and privacy. Various colour coded information zones are set up around the edge of the map. These include: Research, State, Hacking, Security, Tech DIY Education, Privacy and Free Speech Campaigning,

Publishers, Independent Media and Open Infrastructures. Each zone has a numbered list of locations with URLs for relevant web sites and brief descriptions of each site. The number and colour of each entry is also reproduced on the map to show the global position. The map also contains information about radar listening stations and satellites.

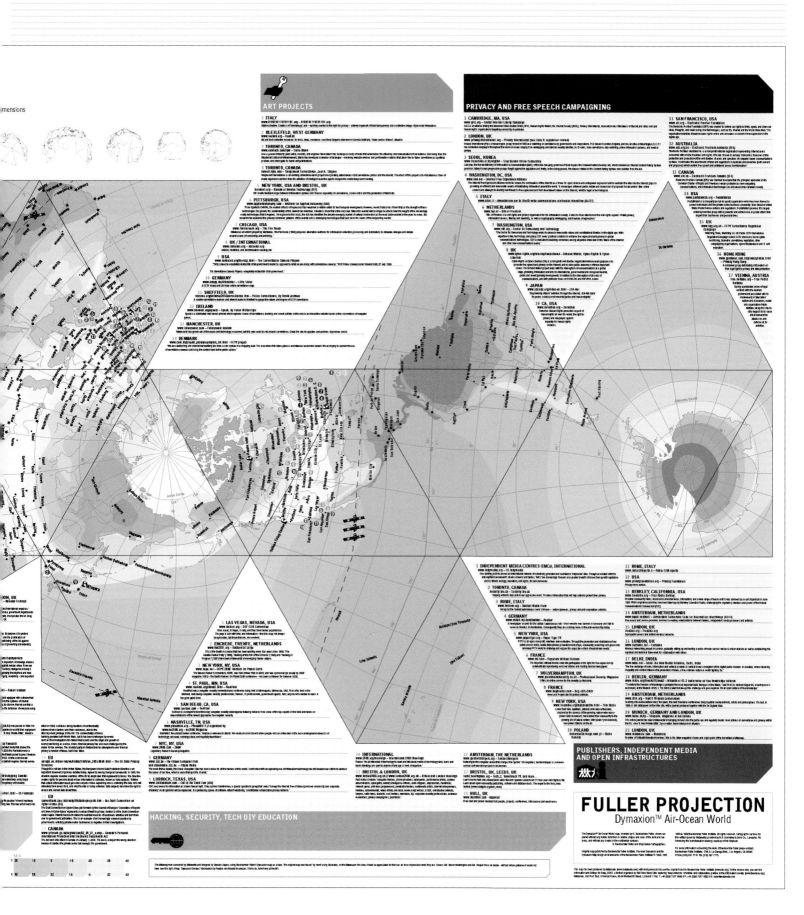

FULLER PROJECTION
Dymaxion™ Air-Ocean World

Design   Lust
Project   Kern DH Map

This map, designed to commemorate the 'Week of Architecture 2000', shows a number of 'year rings' that represent the periods of important growth and development of the city of The Hague. It features a giant satellite photograph of the downtown area. The map includes an extended index, showing the growth in 'structure' and 'mass' of every period, and covers in text and images the most interesting architectural projects and urban development. A colour scheme was designed which assisted in the mapping of these architectural projects in terms of location, the period of their development, and their relationship to the growth in structure and mass.

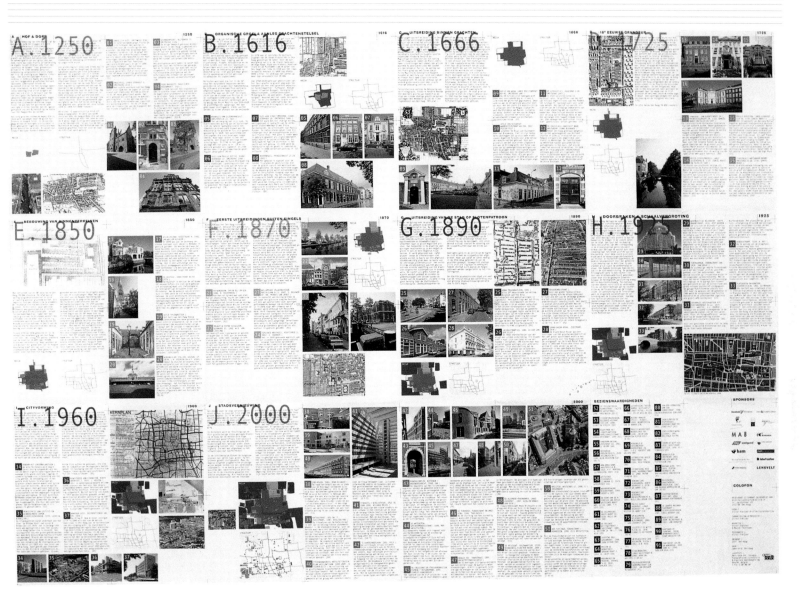

Design   Spin
Project   Recommended Daily Intake poster

20 designers and image makers were asked to design a poster based on the theme of 'Design makes me sick, design makes me well, design makes me complete', organised by Print-run.org for the Roy Castle Lung Cancer Foundation.

Spin's poster analyses the 'recommended daily intake' of various vitamins and minerals, and charts the recommended number of milligrams required. Printed in yellow and black, the poster graphically pulls out information from each of the food supplements in the manner of a periodic table, to create a visually striking poster.

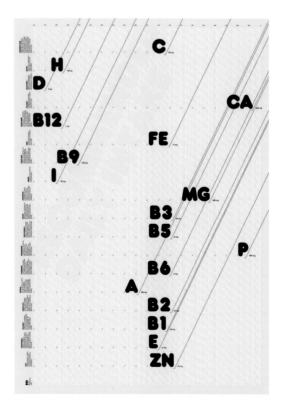

Design   Jeremy Johnson
Project   Colours

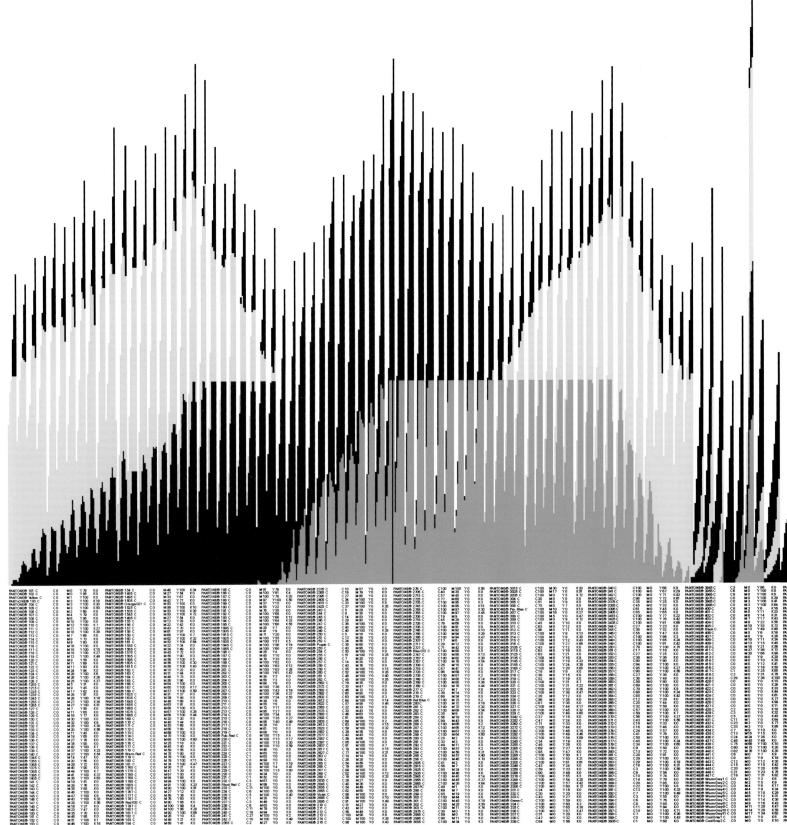

20 designers and image makers were asked to design a poster based on the theme of 'Design makes me sick, design makes me well, design makes me complete', organised by Print-run.org for the Roy Castle Lung Cancer Foundation.

Spin's poster analyses the 'recommended daily intake' of various vitamins and minerals, and charts the recommended number of milligrams required. Printed in yellow and black, the poster graphically pulls out information from each of the food supplements in the manner of a periodic table, to create a visually striking poster.

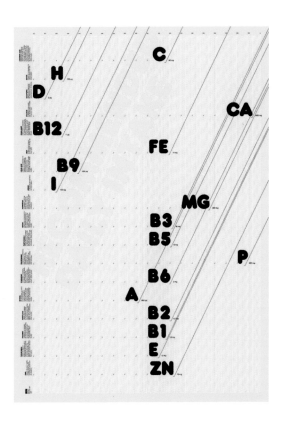

Studio   Sinutype
Design   Maik Stapelberg and Daniel Fritz
Project   AM7/Die Deutsche Flugsicherung Frankfurst/Langen

The 'Akademische Mitteilungen' (Academic Announcements) is a publication of the Academy of Arts and Design Stuttgart, Germany. Issue seven, edited by Daniel Fritz and Maik Stapelberg, two students from the academy, was based around the theme of communication.

This article is about the German air traffic control network, based in Frankfurt/Langen, Germany. The diagram on the left shows the given information from the radar monitor of an air traffic controller which appears only as two-dimensional data. The diagram on the right shows a three-dimensional version of the same data. This view, of course, is left to the imagination of the air traffic controller. The three dimensional version is instantly more approachable, visually representing as it does the altitudes of the various aircraft.

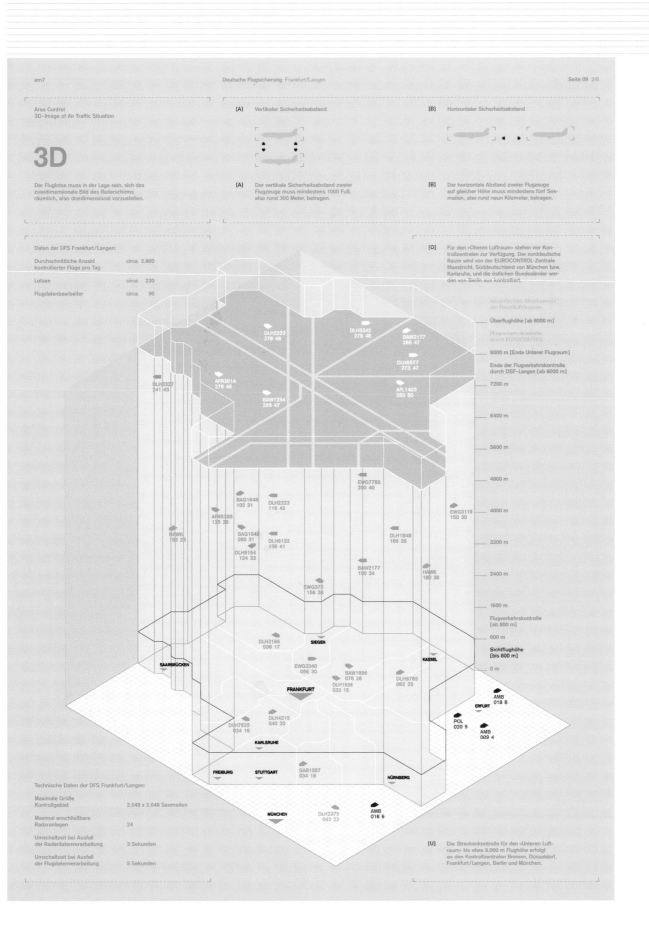

Area Control
3D-Image of Air Traffic Situation

3D

Der Fluglotse muss in der Lage sein, sich das zweidimensionale Bild des Radarschirms räumlich, also dreidimensional vorzustellen.

[A] Vertikaler Sicherheitsabstand

[A] Der vertikale Sicherheitsabstand zweier Flugzeuge muss mindestens 1000 Fuß, also rund 300 Meter, betragen.

[B] Horizontaler Sicherheitsabstand

[B] Der horizontale Abstand zweier Flugzeuge auf gleicher Höhe muss mindestens fünf Seemeilen, also rund neun Kilometer, betragen.

Daten der DFS Frankfurt/Langen:

Durchschnittliche Anzahl kontrollierter Flüge pro Tag	circa 2.800
Lotsen	circa 230
Flugdatenbearbeiter	circa 90

[O] Für den »Oberen Luftraum« stehen vier Kontrollzentralen zur Verfügung. Der norddeutsche Raum wird von der EUROCONTROL-Zentrale Maastricht, Süddeutschland von München bzw. Karlsruhe, und die östlichen Bundesländer werden von Berlin aus kontrolliert.

Vereinfachtes Streckennetz der Hauptluftstraßen

Überflughöhe [ab 8000 m]

Flugverkehrskontrolle durch EUROCONTROL

8000 m [Ende Unterer Flugraum]

Ende der Flugverkehrskontrolle durch DSF-Langen [ab 8000 m]

7200 m

6400 m

5600 m

4800 m

4000 m

3200 m

2400 m

1600 m

Flugverkehrskontrolle [ab 800 m]

800 m

Sichtflughöhe [bis 800 m]

0 m

Technische Daten der DFS Frankfurt/Langen:

Maximale Größe Kontrollgebiet	2.048 x 2.048 Seemeilen
Maximal anschließbare Radaranlagen	24
Umschaltzeit bei Ausfall der Radardatenverarbeitung	3 Sekunden
Umschaltzeit bei Ausfall der Flugdatenverarbeitung	5 Sekunden

[U] Die Streckenkontrolle für den »Unteren Luftraum« bis etwa 8.000 m Flughöhe erfolgt an den Kontrollzentralen Bremen, Düsseldorf, Frankfurt/Langen, Berlin und München.

Design   Jeremy Johnson
Project   Colours

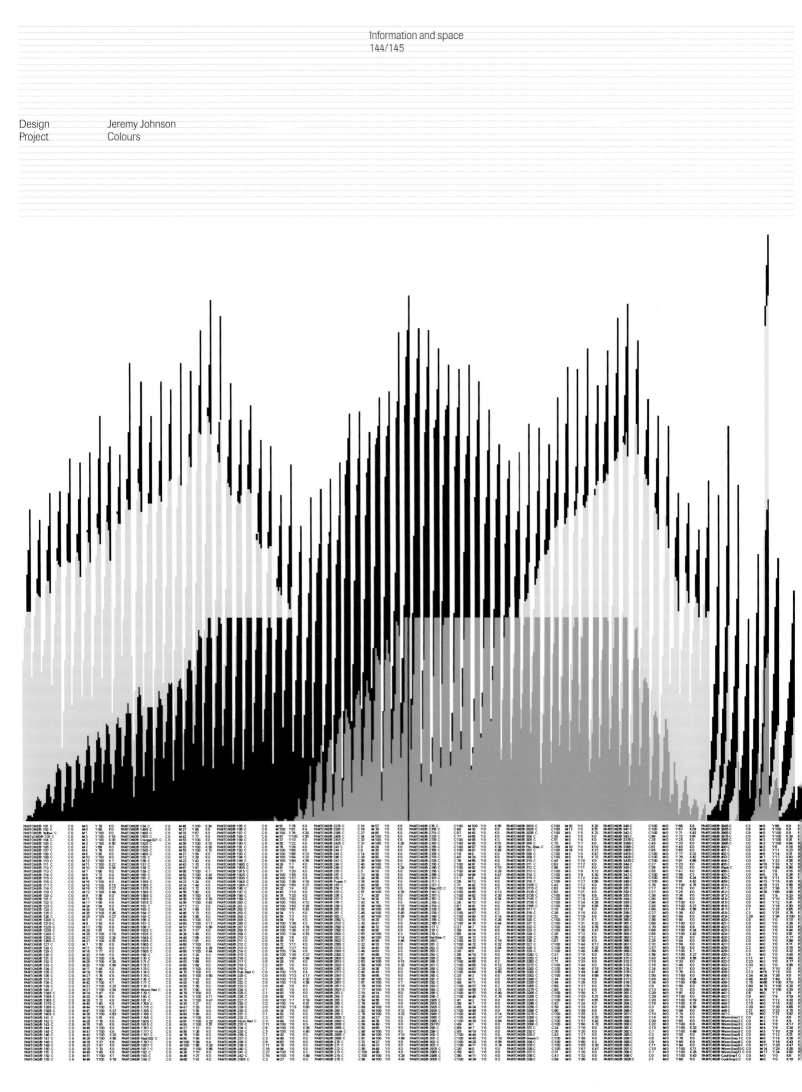

Produced as a self-initiated project, this B1 (27⅘ x 39⅖in)
poster contains the CMYK breakdown for every Pantone
colour, with a graphic representation of each colour shown
purely as a set of four lines (cyan, magenta, yellow and
black). The length of each line is determined by the volume
of colour used in each Pantone equivalent. The mapping
of this information helps the viewer to understand the
quantities and frequencies of process colours used
within special Pantone inks.

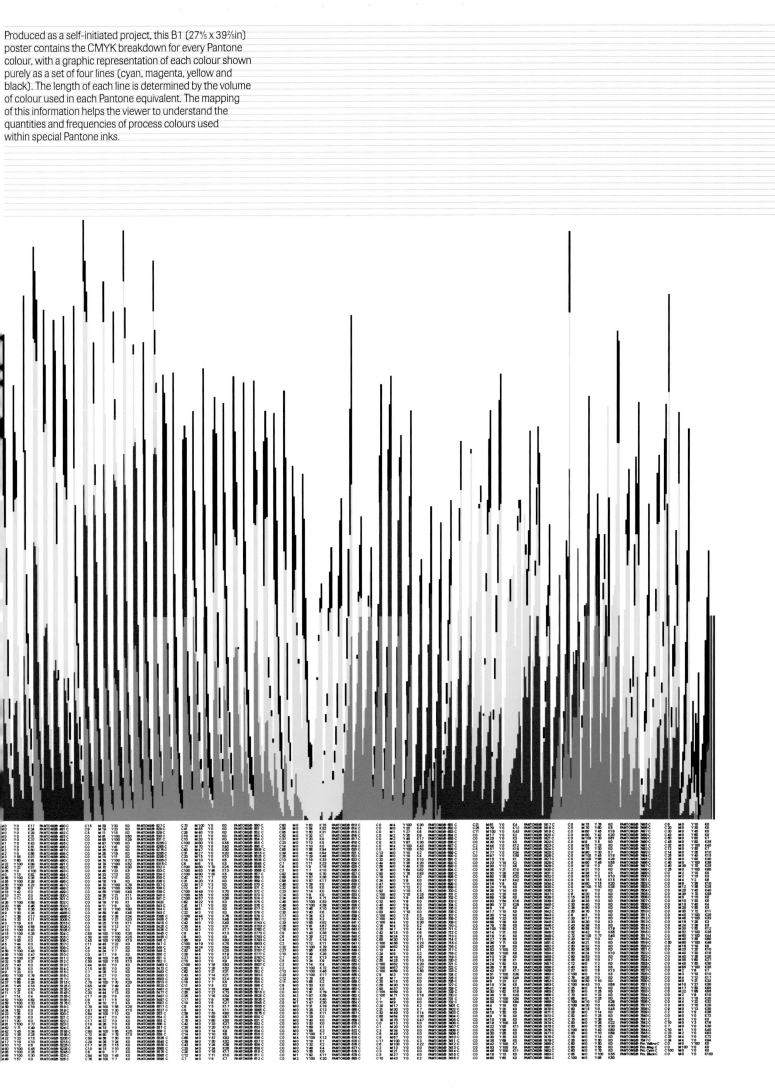

Design   Hochschule für Gestaltung Schwäbisch Gmünd
                Student project
Project   'Arbeitssuche im netz'

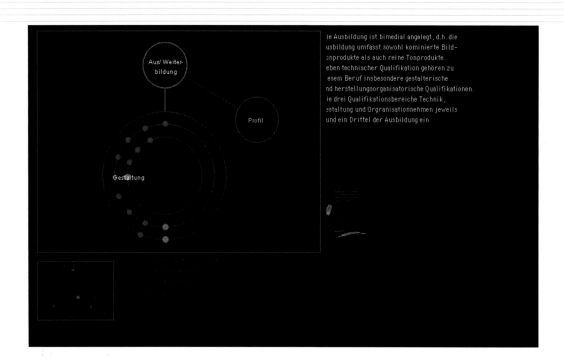

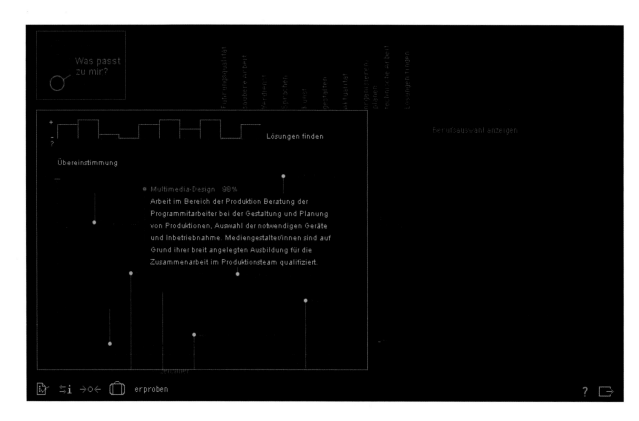

Produced as a project by students at the Hochschule für Gestaltung Schwäbisch Gmünd in Germany, 'Arbeitssuche im netz' is a system to aid job-hunting on-line. The site is aimed at people whose knowledge and skills do not fit in with the traditional criteria set out on many such sites. The site visually illustrates skills-matching and uses a complex indexing system to direct the prospective candidate to the correct area.

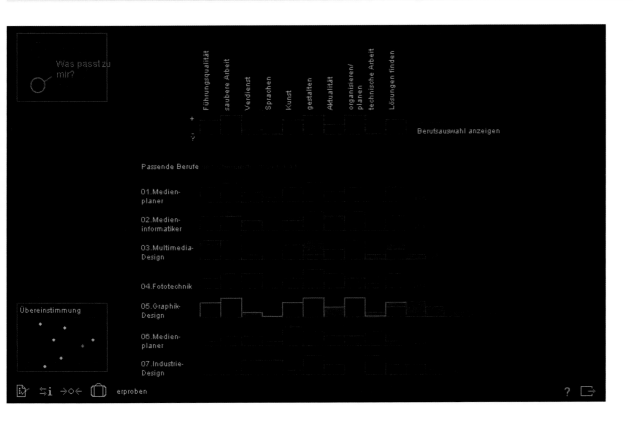

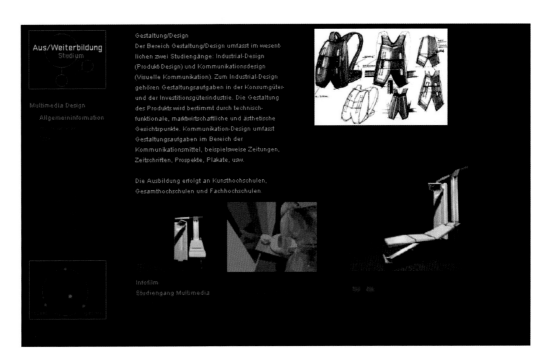

Design	Hochschule für Gestaltung Schwäbisch Gmünd
	Student project
Project	'f.i.n.d.x.'

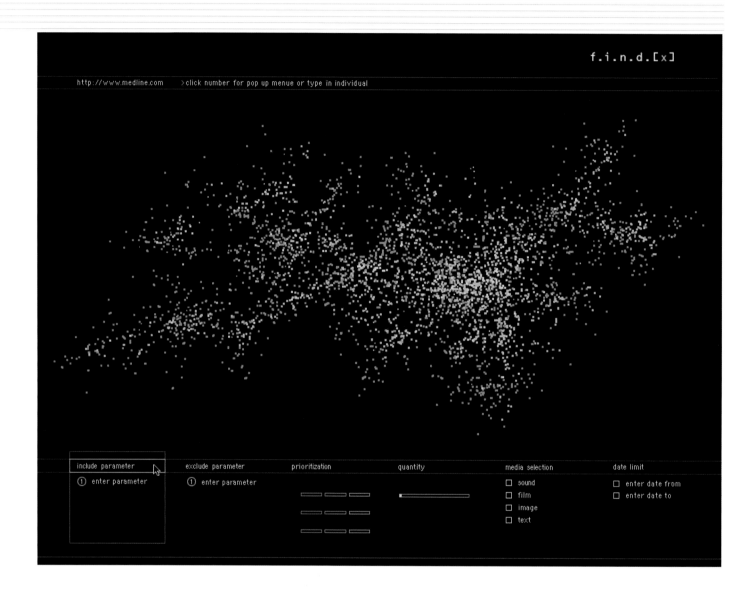

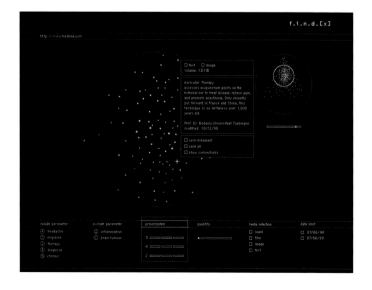

Produced as a project by students at the Hochschule für Gestaltung Schwäbisch Gmünd in Germany, 'f.i.n.d.x.' is a visually-aided investigation instrument for the medical industry. The web site uses as its starting point the chaos of fragmented information that is the Internet, illustrated using hundreds of small green floating squares which form an organic galaxy of information. The user can select areas and zoom in to focus on specific areas of research and information.

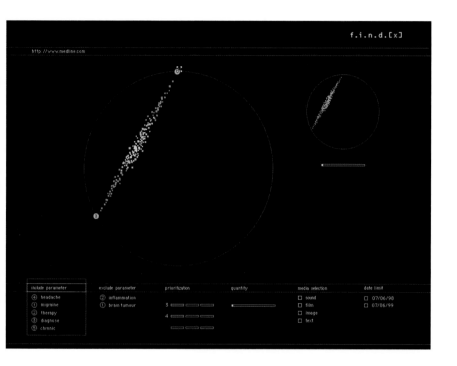

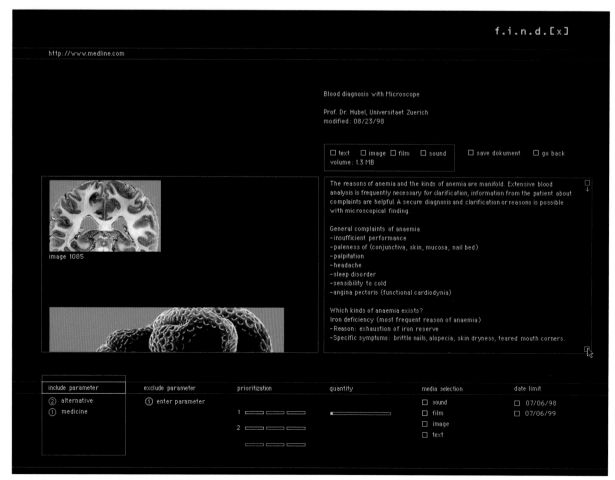

Design   The Attik
Project   Ford 24/7

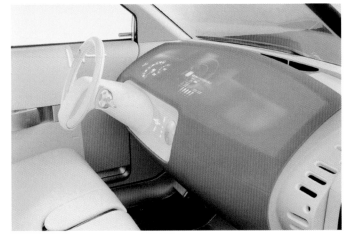

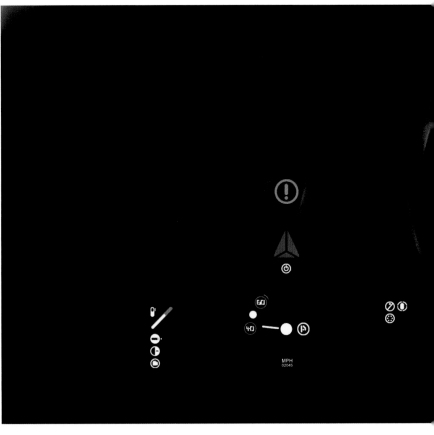

The Ford 24/7 car was one of the highest profile concept cars of recent years. The car was designed by the internationally renowned designer Marc Newson, who conceived the idea of a multi-purpose vehicle that could change its form for different uses. The Attik was commissioned to create an information system that would also revolutionise the traditional car dashboard. The designers' solution was to strip back and remove every knob, button and switch and replace them with a clean curved panel that occupies the full width of the dashboard area. This touch-sensitive panel contains everything necessary for the car's on-board computer system. The information is viewed as a more filmic experience than a conventional touch screen interface, with morphing colours and information which changes according to the operator's requirements, in much the same as the car itself can be customised.

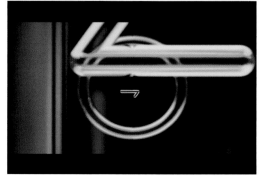

04_Time and space

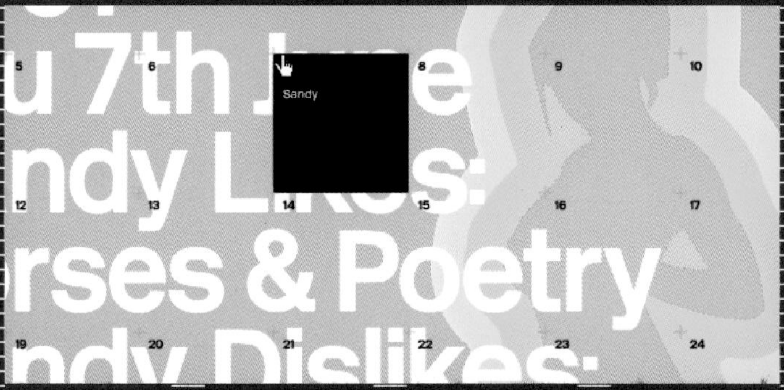

I saw a man he wasn't there

Essay by William Owen
154/155

CNN
GWYNFRYN C
NEW YORK TIMES
MARK HENDE
FBI

ANONYMOUS

FMANJOO@WI

JAMES MERW
R.D. BRIDG

+ PERFORMER
+ THIRSTY WOF
+ GRABBING TV
+ BUZZ ALDRI
+ THE NUMBER

Spin
Twenty-four Hours
188/189

There is a class of maps that plot the things that are not there, that cannot be touched or won't be captured in a single instance. These are maps of information, ideas and organisations; of logical systems of thought, science, business or design; and of change – the mapping of events or actions unfolding over time.

The attraction of mapping intangibles (as opposed to using words or tables to represent them) is that the map can make the relationships of things to one another real and create an intuitive understanding of their dimensions and properties – whether these are concrete, abstract or metaphorical. The graphic language of maps lends itself to representation of the whole of a thing and its parts in a single view, within which we can oscillate rapidly between different levels of detail. Maps allow patterns to emerge and become real, by showing what lies between the visible incidents, artefacts or moments we can otherwise see.

(Information maps are not diagrams. Diagrams are graphic explanations: a map is a graphic representation, although it might explain by inference.)

The importance of mapping intangibles has increased in proportion to the speed of technological and social change. The dematerialisation of products and services and an onrush of excess of choice, facts and demands for our attention results in a disordered and unfamiliar world. In many areas of life the speed of change has created a problem of understanding at the most basic level of what things are, what their value is, who they are for and how to use them. What is lacking is any kind of consensual systemic image of novel objects, organisations or networks. Customers are having difficulty understanding services or product offerings; businesses are changing so rapidly they cannot retain a complete picture of themselves, their operations or of their customers; citizens lack the consistent philosophies or world views that form a foundation for understanding, or the information needed to come to a decision. All of us have difficulty understanding the rate and extent of change itself.

As an aside, it is interesting to note that the last period in which map-making became a popular medium for reorganising thought was in the 16th and 17th centuries. This was the highpoint of the Renaissance and the birth of the modern world, when scientists, alchemists and Rosicruceans attempted to resolve in maps and arcane tables the contradictions between the old world of faith and a new world of rational thought. Their cabalistic maps sought to explain an alternative relationship between man and the universe. Our information maps are more prosaic but are just as much an attempt to extract order from the noise of everyday life.

In commerce, it is difficult to move forward with confidence unless you know where you are today. The mapping of businesses as a precursor to strategic change has become a valuable activity in itself, practised by design companies, IT suppliers and management consultants. The map becomes 'a moment in the process of decision making', a means of possession and control over the enterprise, and a tool for persuasion – part of a business case.

The need to map business has arisen from the rapidly changing boundaries of commerce and the speed of thinking and action required to shift a business back into a competitive position. The rate of change has been driven by a combination of technical development that has automated (or augmented) human activities, and the breakdown of traditional boundaries of business organisations, with looser arrangements of networks of partnerships and short term contractual arrangements replacing strong vertical integration and permanent employee/employer relationships. This looks like a comparatively messy situation, so we map it to find the pattern.

Digital systems promise better business by placing a layer of technology over, or instead of, traditional business practices. Technology has spawned a blizzard of two- and three-letter acronyms – SCM (supply chain management), CM (channel management), KM (knowledge management), DSS (digital self service) CED (customer experience design) and CRM (customer relationship management) – each of which requires an understanding of the relationships, processes and dimensions that are affected. A sensible response is to map the existing and desired situation, and then to identify the gaps.

Businesses are not landscapes, but they do have their own geographies. These are comprised of a host of customer, supplier, regulator, partner and internal relationships; of processes with inputs and outputs, nodal points and directions of flow as well as a beginning and end; of numerous domains of competence of different sizes and characteristics, and diverse dimensions by which the nature and state of the business are monitored.

There is a class of maps that plot things that are not there – logical systems of thought, science, business or design; and change – the mapping of events or actions unfolding over time.

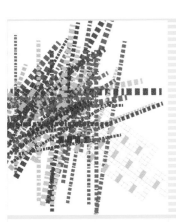

Nina Naegal
and A. Kanna
Time/Emotions
198/199

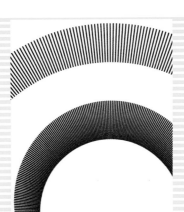

Accept and Proceed
Light and Dark 2008
184/185

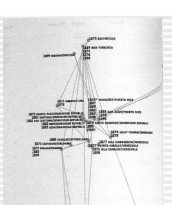

UNA (Amsterdam)
designers
2002 Diary
160/161

The signs and metasigns devised to map physical geography apply themselves well enough to logical systems. Network diagrams illustrate flow and dependencies, matrices show boundaries and absolute size, distribution maps show positions of entities relative to one other – such as competitive position referenced against selected axes or dimensions, and nested signs can represent hierarchies. Maps are particularly useful in revealing how complex activities such as customer interactions work. Businesses touch their customers in many different ways: different parts of a business may be involved in a particular relationship or transaction which may be mediated over multiple channels – shop, phone, SMS, letter, advertisement, etc. It may be critical to a business to understand what is known about a customer at each touchpoint, what value is being exchanged, who the customer is and how they can be characterised usefully and accurately, what is the cost to serve the customer and what is the customer's value over the lifetime of their relationship with the business. The problem is one to which mapping can be applied in order to understand complex patterns of communication and exchange – and to identify contradictory, unwelcome, inefficient or overpriced transactions of whatever kind.

The importance of taxonomy in mapping logical systems, such as this, or when mapping knowledge, cannot be overstated. It is essential to arrive at useful and coherent classifications of things before they can be ordered into their proper place. Inconsistent taxonomy produces a useless map. This is the point, then, at which cartography merges with librarianship and design strategy, and where we arrive at alternatives to standard tabular classifications of books and look instead at pictorial representations of families of information to enable the extraction, viewing and contextual understanding of any kind of symbolic record.

The Internet has created a new class of problem in mapping information. Digitally stored information resolves into a much finer grain than analogue information, reducing down from the book, magazine or journal to the chapter, the article, the image, even the phrase or word. Likewise it no longer has any physical host to provide any kind of 'natural' ordering. This has been highly beneficial, in so far as we can extract information much more quickly in a more convenient form, and we can make connections more quickly wherever a link has been inserted. What we lack, however, is a representation of the entire body of information or a means to rummage around it – with two important exceptions: the catalogue (e.g. Yahoo) and the search engine (e.g. Google). These are of course purely linguistic tools, strictly finite in their nature, smothering serendipity, and sometimes limited to the point of stupidity in understanding what it is we are really looking for.

The alternative to linguistic search is a graphical interface that may allow for less exact but ultimately more successful investigations. A highly successful example is Smartmoney's 'Map of the Market' (a chloropleth map of the market capitalisation of Fortune 500 companies that changes dynamically with the stock price). This is a graphical representation that gives a genuinely useful overview of states and trends combined with detailed information, interrogated by a graphic interface.

The Map of the Market succeeds because it layers information in two dimensions and uses a consistent taxonomy to divide the layers and a design strategy that reveals the dynamic quality of the activity it represents. Everything necessary to obtain an overview is visible simultaneously and in the correct proportion and state.

This essay, however, ends with an acknowledgement of failure. Most designers who have attempted to represent Internet-based information have produced maps that show nothing but network flows or nested texts. These maps have failed to replicate, in even the most rudimentary way, the sensory representation (and the massive boost to the memory and the imagination) one receives on entering a library and seeing, smelling and feeling the books on the shelf. One of the reasons for this failure has been an obsession with 3D perspective within the computer-oriented section of the design community. The idea that a perspectival simulation of the physical world will help us understand digital information is a fallacy, because perspective limits viewpoint and imposes distance where none exists. For proof, visit Cyberatlas.com, where there are numerous representations of the Internet in three dimensions that tell us nothing at all about what is there.

Design   UNA (Amsterdam) designers / UNA (London) designers
Project   Diary
Photography Anthony Oliver

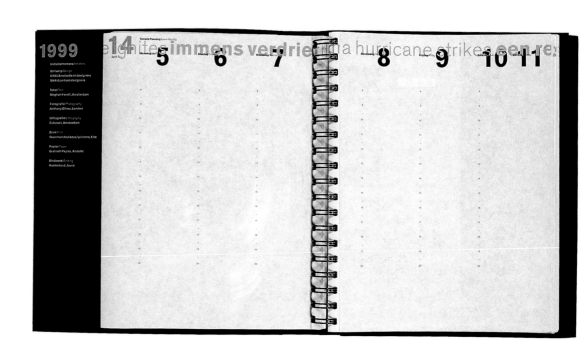

Dutch design consultancy UNA produced a double-year edition diary for 1999 and 2000, as a way of connecting the two centuries. An elaborate folding system was employed enabling the correct year to be visible. The diary has two covers, the first cover titled 'two thousand -1' and the second cover entitled 'nineteen ninety nine +1'. For 1999 the pages work quite conventionally, however at the turn of the century, the pages of the diary have to be turned back on themselves to reveal the new dates, and a fresh selection of photographs.

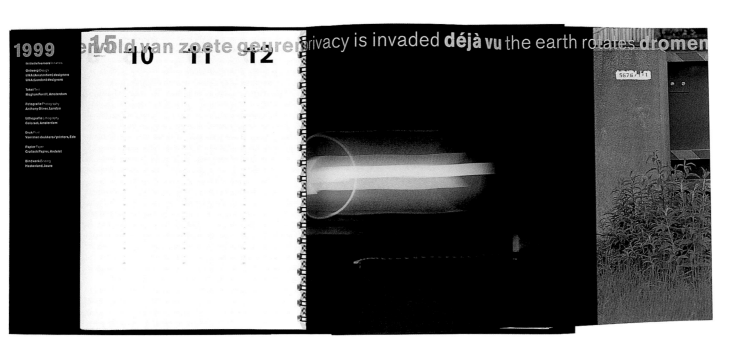

Design   UNA (Amsterdam) designers
Project   Diary

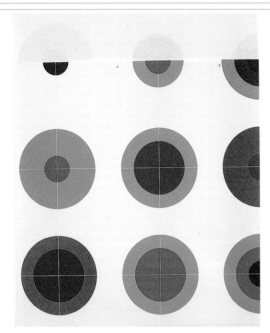

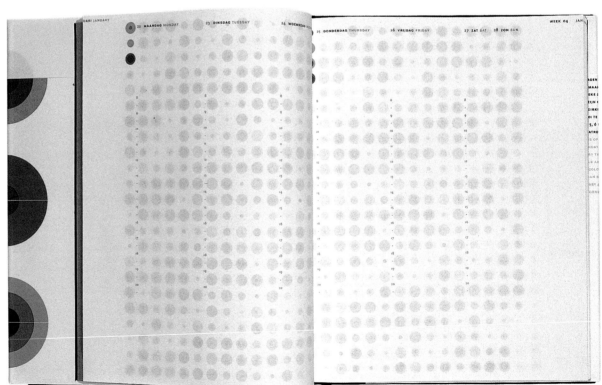

Many recipients of UNA's 2001 diary found it almost too beautiful to use. The quality and attention to detail present in this book is outstanding, as is the complexity of the idea and system behind the design. As stated on the back of the dust jacket: 'The 365 days of the year are divided into 12 months. each month naturally has a first, a second, a third, a fourth and sometimes a fifth Monday, Tuesday, Wednesday, Thursday, Friday, Saturday and Sunday.
                    In this diary these particular days are coded by a unique symbol, which means that there is a total of 35 different symbols. The symbols are constructed by overprinting up to three varying sized concentric circles, in a combination of one of three different colours. On the page where January 1, 2 and 3 appear, the complete pattern of circles representing the 365 days of the year 2001 can be seen. The pattern is in fact mirror printed on the reverse side of the Japanese-folded sheet. On the following page, January 4, 5, 6 and 7, the symbols have moved three positions forward. This twice weekly rhythm continues throughout the diary. Consequently the empty space grows from the bottom right of the page and the year 2001 gradually disappears.'

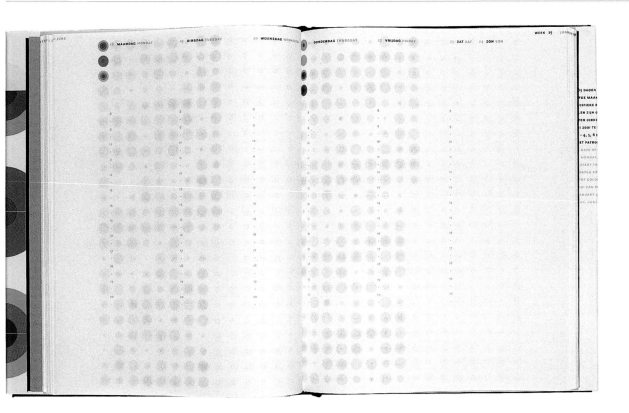

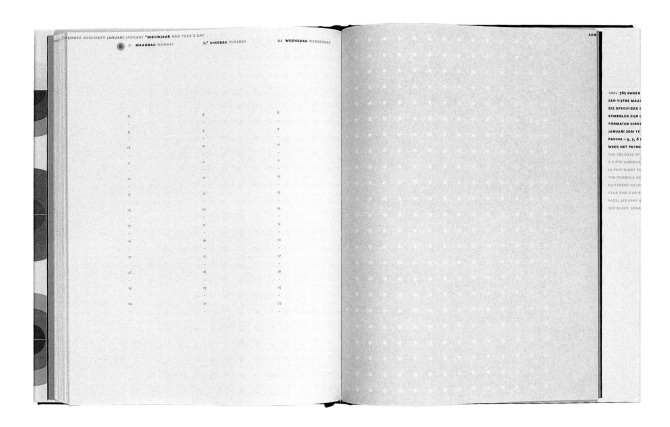

Design   UNA (Amsterdam) designers
Project   Diary

Dutch design consultancy UNA's 2002 diary sets out on a mission to find a significant event globally for each day of the year. The diary, as with previous UNA diaries, represents a significant typographic achievement and, through its printing, exudes quality. As in previous examples, the designers have used folded sheets – French-folded in this case – to allow subtle images to appear. The dates, together with information about special events, occasions and festivals, are printed on the face of the sheet, while icons and images pertinent to the particular event are printed inside the French-fold. The pages are perforated along the French-fold edge, allowing the user to easily tear open the sleeve to better access the additional information.

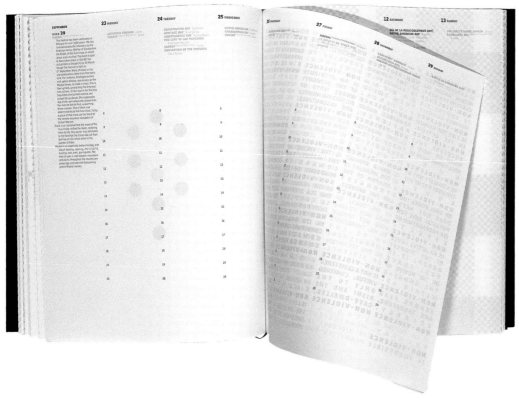

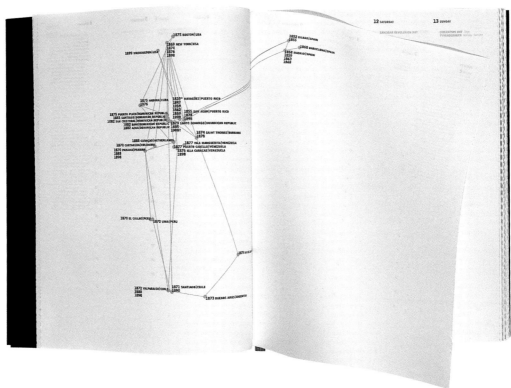

Design   A.G. Fronzoni
Project   365 diary

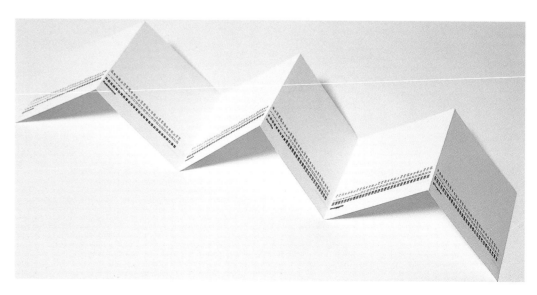

This pocket-sized diary by the Italian designer A.G. Fronzoni only measures 3¾ x 3⁹⁄₆₄in (95 x 80mm), but with over 600 pages is 1½in (38mm) thick. Unusually, the diary can be used in any year as the only information it contains is the day of the year running from 1 (1st of January) to 365 (31st of December). Every page works the digits into a different form and as the pages are printed onto thin paper the preceding and following page numbers are just visible, which makes the diary even richer. The book is accompanied by a small 12-page concertina-folded leaflet with a month on each page, in which again, the 365 days of the year are listed in one continuous line, with the day and date information running adjacent to it.

Design   Irwin Glusker
Project   Phases of the Moon 2000

Although not the first or only example of a lunar-related calendar, this example from the Museum of Modern Art in New York is simple, beautiful, effective, and clearly works as a conventional calendar with each progressive crescent of the moon shown for each day of the month. The calendar is finely printed with each moon crafted with a full circle in a spot UV varnish and the crescent printed white out.

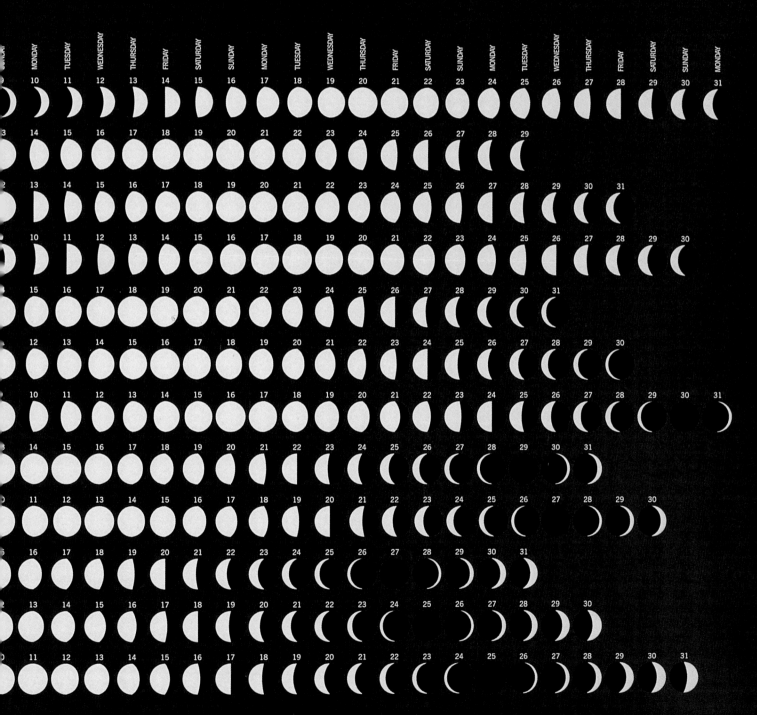

Design   Büro für Gestaltung
Project   Calendars 1998–2001

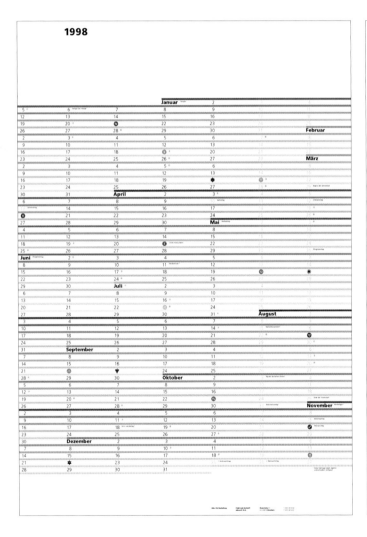

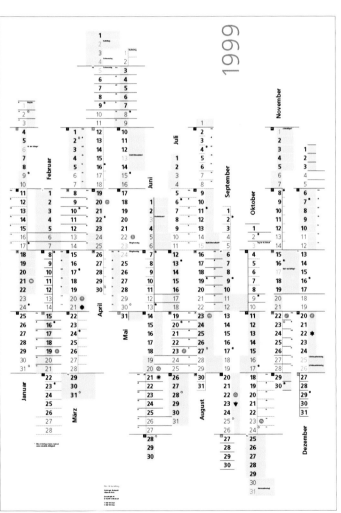

Produced as an ongoing self-initiated project to research
the structure that lies behind the 365 days, 52 weeks
and 12 months of the year, the aim is to find a different
solution each year. The designers were less interested in
the final visual appearance of the poster, and were mainly
concerned with the process. Each poster measures 33⁵/₆₄ x
23⅝in (840 x 600mm) and is reproduced in full colour.
The calendars are always typographic, working purely with
the given numerical data of the calendar.

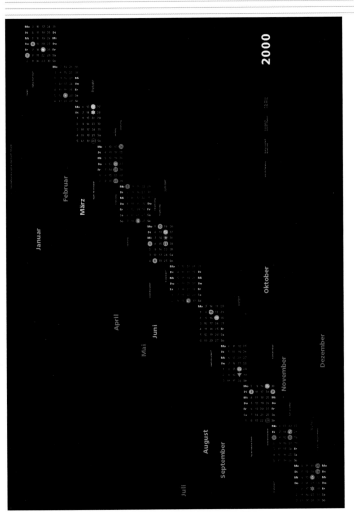

Design   Secondary Modern
Project   'Rokeby Venus'

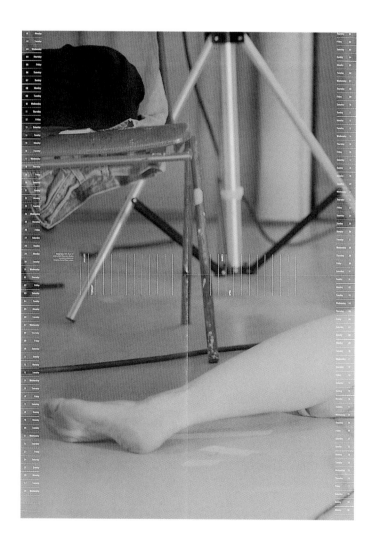

Design   Proctor and Stevenson
Project   Calendar

When the UK-based graphic design consultancy NB: Studio was commissioned by the furniture company Knoll International to produce a promotional calendar, the designers' response was this elegant poster. The months are set out in a conventional manner as are the dates within each month. The names of days, however, are replaced with the names of furniture designers and the names of famous pieces of Knoll furniture. Above this information is a keyline drawing of each classic piece of furniture. For weekends, a single sofa extends over the two-day period.

Design   NB:Studio
Project   Knoll calendar – Twenty-First Century Classics

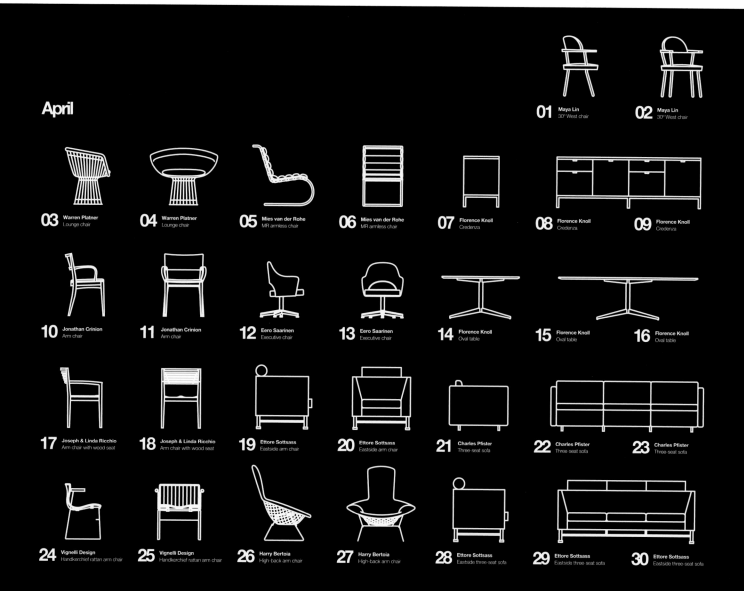

April

01 **Maya Lin**
30° West chair

02 **Maya Lin**
30° West chair

03 **Warren Platner**
Lounge chair

04 **Warren Platner**
Lounge chair

05 **Mies van der Rohe**
MR armless chair

06 **Mies van der Rohe**
MR armless chair

07 **Florence Knoll**
Credenza

08 **Florence Knoll**
Credenza

09 **Florence Knoll**
Credenza

10 **Jonathan Crinion**
Arm chair

11 **Jonathan Crinion**
Arm chair

12 **Eero Saarinen**
Executive chair

13 **Eero Saarinen**
Executive chair

14 **Florence Knoll**
Oval table

15 **Florence Knoll**
Oval table

16 **Florence Knoll**
Oval table

17 **Joseph & Linda Ricchio**
Arm chair with wood seat

18 **Joseph & Linda Ricchio**
Arm chair with wood seat

19 **Ettore Sottsass**
Eastside arm chair

20 **Ettore Sottsass**
Eastside arm chair

21 **Charles Pfister**
Three-seat sofa

22 **Charles Pfister**
Three-seat sofa

23 **Charles Pfister**
Three-seat sofa

24 **Vignelli Design**
Handkerchief rattan arm chair

25 **Vignelli Design**
Handkerchief rattan arm chair

26 **Harry Bertoia**
High-back arm chair

27 **Harry Bertoia**
High-back arm chair

28 **Ettore Sottsass**
Eastside three-seat sofa

29 **Ettore Sottsass**
Eastside three-seat sofa

30 **Ettore Sottsass**
Eastside three-seat sofa

Produced as a set of three A2 (16½ x 23⅔in) posters folded down to A4 (8³⁄₁₀ x 11⁷⁄₁₀in) and enclosed in a clear plastic sleeve, the designers of this piece are exploring a theme introduced by themselves in 1998, and continued each year since (the calendar shown is for 2001). The typography changes from year to year, as does the content. The 1998 calendar utilised colour photographs of skyscrapers shot through the window of an aeroplane. Their 1999 version reduced the work to pure typography, set in a similar manner to the calendar shown. The 2000 calendar used a large, detailed line drawing of an urban landscape.

This calendar works as a triptych in the classic sense. Entitled 'Rokeby Venus', the nude study is a self-portrait by Jemima Stehli set-up as a transcription of the famous painting by Velazquez, c1647. The only difference is that the cupid in the original has been replaced with photographic studio equipment. The calendar data works as follows: every two months run down a single column on each long edge of the posters. A series of 13 vertical rules runs horizontally across half of each poster; within these rules is positioned the relevant month.

The Bristol, UK-based design company Proctor and Stevenson produced this A3 (11⅞₁₀ x 16½in) calendar. Each month, which was made up of two A3 pages, was given to a different designer within the company, which created a variety of responses within a single design piece.
        April (shown here) was designed by Ben Tappenden. The first page maps out the design company's offices by showing the view out of every window in the building. Each image is credited with the name of the designer who sits by the window it represents. These photographs are positioned in rows according to the positions of the windows within the building – the top

row is the third floor, the bottom row is the ground floor. A thin colour bar runs along one edge of each image to denote the orientation of the window – east is represented by a yellow strip on the right edge, south by an orange strip on the bottom edge, west by a green strip on the left edge.
        The second page of April contains the dates for the month with an aerial satellite photograph of the area the company's building is located within, together with a series of detailed images showing fragments of the surrounding environment.

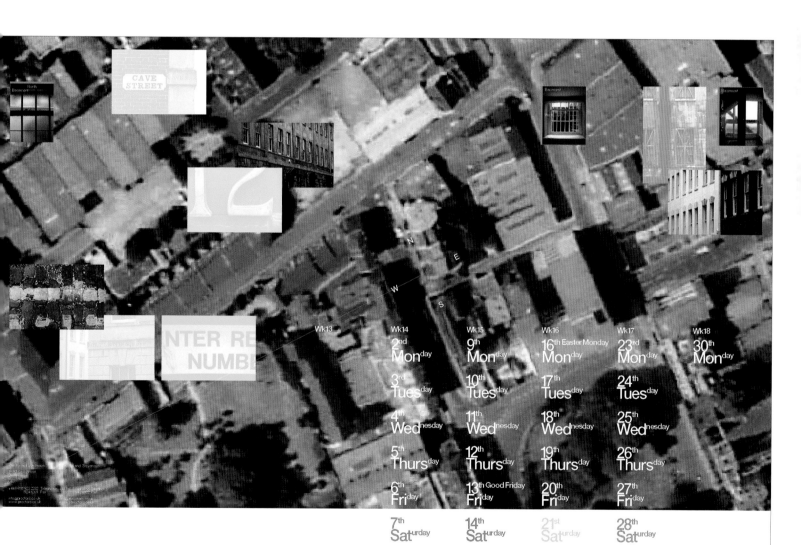

Design	Struktur Design		Design	Struktur Design
Project	1998 Kalendar		Project	Seven Days 1999

1998

	January	February	March	April	May	June	July	August	September	October	November	December
01	Thursday	Sunday	Sunday	Wednesday	Friday	Monday	Wednesday	Saturday	Tuesday	Thursday	Sunday	Tuesday
02	Friday	Monday	Monday	Thursday	Saturday	Tuesday	Thursday	Sunday	Wednesday	Friday	Monday	Wednesday
03	Saturday	Tuesday	Tuesday	Friday	Sunday	Wednesday	Friday	Monday	Thursday	Saturday	Tuesday	Thursday
04	Sunday	Wednesday	Wednesday	Saturday	Monday	Thursday	Saturday	Tuesday	Friday	Sunday	Wednesday	Friday
05	Monday	Thursday	Thursday	Sunday	Tuesday	Friday	Sunday	Wednesday	Saturday	Monday	Thursday	Saturday
06	Tuesday	Friday	Friday	Monday	Wednesday	Saturday	Monday	Thursday	Sunday	Tuesday	Friday	Sunday
07	Wednesday	Saturday	Saturday	Tuesday	Thursday	Sunday	Tuesday	Friday	Monday	Wednesday	Saturday	Monday
08	Thursday	Sunday	Sunday	Wednesday	Friday	Monday	Wednesday	Saturday	Tuesday	Thursday	Sunday	Tuesday
09	Friday	Monday	Monday	Thursday	Saturday	Tuesday	Thursday	Sunday	Wednesday	Friday	Monday	Wednesday
10	Saturday	Tuesday	Tuesday	Friday	Sunday	Wednesday	Friday	Monday	Thursday	Saturday	Tuesday	Thursday
11	Sunday	Wednesday	Wednesday	Saturday	Monday	Thursday	Saturday	Tuesday	Friday	Sunday	Wednesday	Friday
12	Monday	Thursday	Thursday	Sunday	Tuesday	Friday	Sunday	Wednesday	Saturday	Monday	Thursday	Saturday
13	Tuesday	Friday	Friday	Monday	Wednesday	Saturday	Monday	Thursday	Sunday	Tuesday	Friday	Sunday
14	Wednesday	Saturday	Saturday	Tuesday	Thursday	Sunday	Tuesday	Friday	Monday	Wednesday	Saturday	Monday
15	Thursday	Sunday	Sunday	Wednesday	Friday	Monday	Wednesday	Saturday	Tuesday	Thursday	Sunday	Tuesday
16	Friday	Monday	Monday	Thursday	Saturday	Tuesday	Thursday	Sunday	Wednesday	Friday	Monday	Wednesday
17	Saturday	Tuesday	Tuesday	Friday	Sunday	Wednesday	Friday	Monday	Thursday	Saturday	Tuesday	Thursday
18	Sunday	Wednesday	Wednesday	Saturday	Monday	Thursday	Saturday	Tuesday	Friday	Sunday	Wednesday	Friday
19	Monday	Thursday	Thursday	Sunday	Tuesday	Friday	Sunday	Wednesday	Saturday	Monday	Thursday	Saturday
20	Tuesday	Friday	Friday	Monday	Wednesday	Saturday	Monday	Thursday	Sunday	Tuesday	Friday	Sunday
21	Wednesday	Saturday	Saturday	Tuesday	Thursday	Sunday	Tuesday	Friday	Monday	Wednesday	Saturday	Monday
22	Thursday	Sunday	Sunday	Wednesday	Friday	Monday	Wednesday	Saturday	Tuesday	Thursday	Sunday	Tuesday
23	Friday	Monday	Monday	Thursday	Saturday	Tuesday	Thursday	Sunday	Wednesday	Friday	Monday	Wednesday
24	Saturday	Tuesday	Tuesday	Friday	Sunday	Wednesday	Friday	Monday	Thursday	Saturday	Tuesday	Thursday
25	Sunday	Wednesday	Wednesday	Saturday	Monday	Thursday	Saturday	Tuesday	Friday	Sunday	Wednesday	Friday
26	Monday	Thursday	Thursday	Sunday	Tuesday	Friday	Sunday	Wednesday	Saturday	Monday	Thursday	Saturday
27	Tuesday	Friday	Friday	Monday	Wednesday	Saturday	Monday	Thursday	Sunday	Tuesday	Friday	Sunday
28	Wednesday	Saturday	Saturday	Tuesday	Thursday	Sunday	Tuesday	Friday	Monday	Wednesday	Saturday	Monday
29	Thursday		Sunday	Wednesday	Friday	Monday	Wednesday	Saturday	Tuesday	Thursday	Sunday	Tuesday
30	Friday		Monday	Thursday	Saturday	Tuesday	Thursday	Sunday	Wednesday	Friday	Monday	Wednesday
31	Saturday		Tuesday		Sunday		Friday	Monday		Saturday		Thursday

Working with a given set of information – the days and dates of the year – Struktur tried to re-organise the data in an unconventional manner. For the 1998 calendar, an A2 (16½ x 23⅝in) poster showing the entire year was chosen as the platform. Working with the principle that there are a maximum of 31 days in any given month, the hierarchy of the calender shifted from the prominence usually given to the months to the days of the month, from 1 through to 31. The individual days of the year are listed in columns, with weekends printed white out of the background colour.

The 1999 calendar took the form of a desk diary, and in a development from the previous year, the information was re-structured grouping all the Mondays on one page, followed by all the Tuesdays, and so on, thus creating a daily calendar. At the back of the calendar is a page featuring public holidays, a vacation page, which contains all the days of the year, so the user can highlight personal holiday times, and finally a page called 'lunch', adding a time based element to the day.

The grid system present on each page is a graphic chart of each day of the year: the first column is January, the second column is February. On each page, the given day is represented with a white box, so on Monday,

the chart shows white boxes for every Monday throughout the year. The colour palette uses the basic process colours – cyan, magenta, yellow and black – with each day using a combination of the two colours, working like a printer's tint book, starting with the first of January in 3 per cent of each colour, going through to the 31st of December printed in 100 per cent of each colour.

The white keyline grid that separates each of the boxes becomes increasingly thick as one journeys through the week until by Sunday, the white lines become thicker than the boxes, visually referring to the end of the week.

seven days

Struktur Design's 1999 kalendar

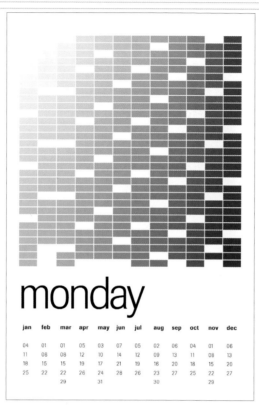

monday

jan	feb	mar	apr	may	jun	jul	aug	sep	oct	nov	dec
04	01	01	05	03	07	05	02	06	04	01	06
11	08	08	12	10	14	12	09	13	11	08	13
18	15	15	19	17	21	19	16	20	18	15	20
25	22	22	26	24	28	26	23	27	25	22	27
		29		31			30			29	

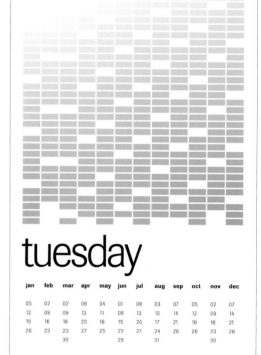

tuesday

jan	feb	mar	apr	may	jun	jul	aug	sep	oct	nov	dec
05	02	02	06	04	01	06	03	07	05	02	07
12	09	09	13	11	08	13	10	14	12	09	14
19	16	16	20	18	15	20	17	21	19	16	21
26	23	23	27	25	22	27	24	28	26	23	28
		30			29		31			30	

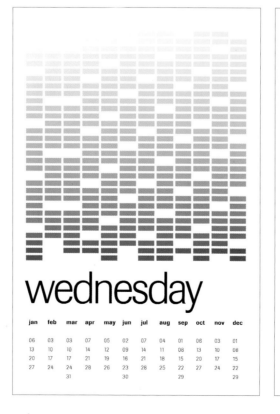

wednesday

jan	feb	mar	apr	may	jun	jul	aug	sep	oct	nov	dec
06	03	03	07	05	02	07	04	01	06	03	01
13	10	10	14	12	09	14	11	08	13	10	08
20	17	17	21	19	16	21	18	15	20	17	15
27	24	24	28	26	23	28	25	22	27	24	22
		31			30			29			29

thursday

jan	feb	mar	apr	may	jun	jul	aug	sep	oct	nov	dec
07	04	04	01	06	03	01	05	02	07	04	02
14	11	11	08	13	10	08	12	09	14	11	09
21	18	18	15	20	17	15	19	16	21	18	16
28	25	25	22	27	24	22	26	23	28	25	23
			29			29		30			30

Design	Struktur Design
Project	Perpetual Kalendar

Design	Struktur Design
Project	Twentyfour Hour Clock

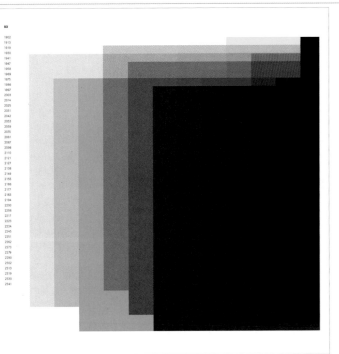

03
1902 1913 1919 1930 1941 1947 1958 1969 1975 1986 1997 2003 2014 2025 2031 2042 2053 2059 2070 2081 2087 2098 2110 2121 2127 2138 2149 2155 2166 2177 2194 2206 2217 2223 2234 2245 2251 2262 2273 2279 2290 2302 2313 2319 2330 2341

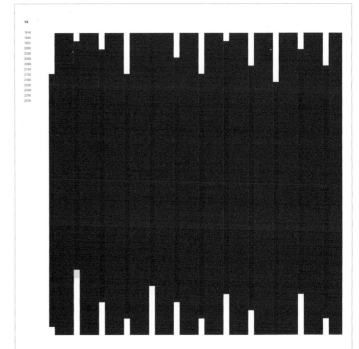

13
1916 1944 1972 2000 2028 2056 2084 2124 2152 2180 2220 2248 2276 2316

03	January	February	March	April	May	June	July	August	September	October	November	December
Monday									01			01
Tuesday				01			01		02			02
Wednesday	01			02			02		03	01		03
Thursday	02			03	01		03		04	02		04
Friday	03			04	02		04	01	05	03		05
Saturday	04	01	01	05	03		05	02	06	04	01	06
Sunday	05	02	02	06	04	01	06	03	07	05	02	07
Monday	06	03	03	07	05	02	07	04	08	06	03	08
Tuesday	07	04	04	08	06	03	08	05	09	07	04	09
Wednesday	08	05	05	09	07	04	09	06	10	08	05	10
Thursday	09	06	06	10	08	05	10	07	11	09	06	11
Friday	10	07	07	11	09	06	11	08	12	10	07	12
Saturday	11	08	08	12	10	07	12	09	13	11	08	13
Sunday	12	09	09	13	11	08	13	10	14	12	09	14
Monday	13	10	10	14	12	09	14	11	15	13	10	15
Tuesday	14	11	11	15	13	10	15	12	16	14	11	16
Wednesday	15	12	12	16	14	11	16	13	17	15	12	17
Thursday	16	13	13	17	15	12	17	14	18	16	13	18
Friday	17	14	14	18	16	13	18	15	19	17	14	19
Saturday	18	15	15	19	17	14	19	16	20	18	15	20
Sunday	19	16	16	20	18	15	20	17	21	19	16	21
Monday	20	17	17	21	19	16	21	18	22	20	17	22
Tuesday	21	18	18	22	20	17	22	19	23	21	18	23
Wednesday	22	19	19	23	21	18	23	20	24	22	19	24
Thursday	23	20	20	24	22	19	24	21	25	23	20	25
Friday	24	21	21	25	23	20	25	22	26	24	21	26
Saturday	25	22	22	26	24	21	26	23	27	25	22	27
Sunday	26	23	23	27	25	22	27	24	28	26	23	28
Monday	27	24	24	28	26	23	28	25	29	27	24	29
Tuesday	28	25	25	29	27	24	29	26	30	28	25	30
Wednesday	29	26	26	30	28	25	30	27		29	26	31
Thursday	30	27	27		29	26	31	28		30	27	
Friday	31	28	28		30	27		29		31	28	
Saturday			29		31	28		30			29	
Sunday			30			29		31			30	
Monday			31			30						
Tuesday												

13	January	February	March	April	May	June	July	August	September	October	November	December
Monday					01							
Tuesday		01			02			01				
Wednesday		02	01		03			02			01	
Thursday		03	02		04	01		03			02	
Friday		04	03		05	02		04	01		03	01
Saturday	01	05	04	01	06	03	01	05	02		04	02
Sunday	02	06	05	02	07	04	02	06	03	01	05	03
Monday	03	07	06	03	08	05	03	07	04	02	06	04
Tuesday	04	08	07	04	09	06	04	08	05	03	07	05
Wednesday	05	09	08	05	10	07	05	09	06	04	08	06
Thursday	06	10	09	06	11	08	06	10	07	05	09	07
Friday	07	11	10	07	12	09	07	11	08	06	10	08
Saturday	08	12	11	08	13	10	08	12	09	07	11	09
Sunday	09	13	12	09	14	11	09	13	10	08	12	10
Monday	10	14	13	10	15	12	10	14	11	09	13	11
Tuesday	11	15	14	11	16	13	11	15	12	10	14	12
Wednesday	12	16	15	12	17	14	12	16	13	11	15	13
Thursday	13	17	16	13	18	15	13	17	14	12	16	14
Friday	14	18	17	14	19	16	14	18	15	13	17	15
Saturday	15	19	18	15	20	17	15	19	16	14	18	16
Sunday	16	20	19	16	21	18	16	20	17	15	19	17
Monday	17	21	20	17	22	19	17	21	18	16	20	18
Tuesday	18	22	21	18	23	20	18	22	19	17	21	19
Wednesday	19	23	22	19	24	21	19	23	20	18	22	20
Thursday	20	24	23	20	25	22	20	24	21	19	23	21
Friday	21	25	24	21	26	23	21	25	22	20	24	22
Saturday	22	26	25	22	27	24	22	26	23	21	25	23
Sunday	23	27	26	23	28	25	23	27	24	22	26	24
Monday	24	28	27	24	29	26	24	28	25	23	27	25
Tuesday	25	29	28	25	30	27	25	29	26	24	28	26
Wednesday	26		29	26	31	28	26	30	27	25	29	27
Thursday	27		30	27		29	27	31	28	26	30	28
Friday	28		31	28		30	28		29	27		29
Saturday	29			29			29		30	28		30
Sunday	30			30			30			29		31
Monday	31						31			30		
Tuesday										31		

Produced at the end of the 20th century, the Perpetual Kalendar effectively completed Struktur's series of calendars, as this calendar can be used for every year from 1900 to 2343. The single publication contains 14 permutations of the calendar, which allows for every variation of the day/date sequence – 1st of January can fall on a Monday, Tuesday, Wednesday etc. (seven versions), and the day/date sequence alters every leap year, requiring a further seven variations.

Each spread from the calendar shows a full year, working as a clear typographic page and an illustrative page, based on the inherent grid system and flow of dates. A list of the relevant years appears down the side of each spread for ease of use.

Twentyfour Hour Clock was produced as a result of an open brief set by the London-based specialist printer Artomatic. The A2 (16½ x 23⅝in) silkscreen printed poster was designed as part of an ongoing research project looking at time systems, and works as a direct extension of the Struktur Design calendars and diaries (see pages 176/177/178). The poster sets out every second, minute and hour of a 24-hour period, with each time measuring unit reproduced in progressively larger point sizes.

| Design | Struktur Design |
| Project | Minutes diary |

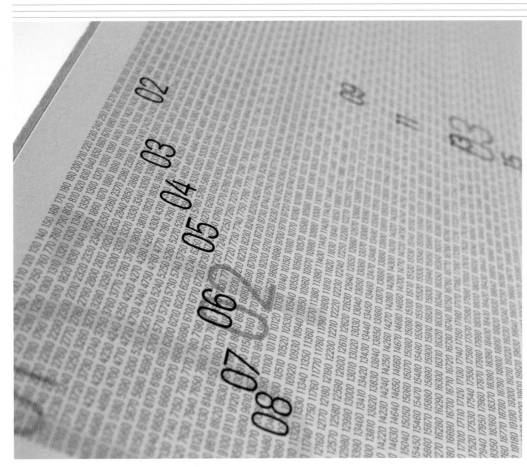

The concertina-folded pages of this diary extend to almost 19¹¹⁄₁₆ft (6 metres) in length. The year is broken down into its consituent minutes, all 525,600 of them set at 10-minute intervals, which are printed in fluorescent pink continuously over the pages. A line return is the only indication of change within this sea of numbers. This small-scale data is overprinted with the days of the year, 1–365 in black. The weeks are highlighted in a warm grey, and finally the months are indicated much larger in a pale tint of grey. The rhythmic nature of the numerical sequence plays a key part in the appearance of the work.

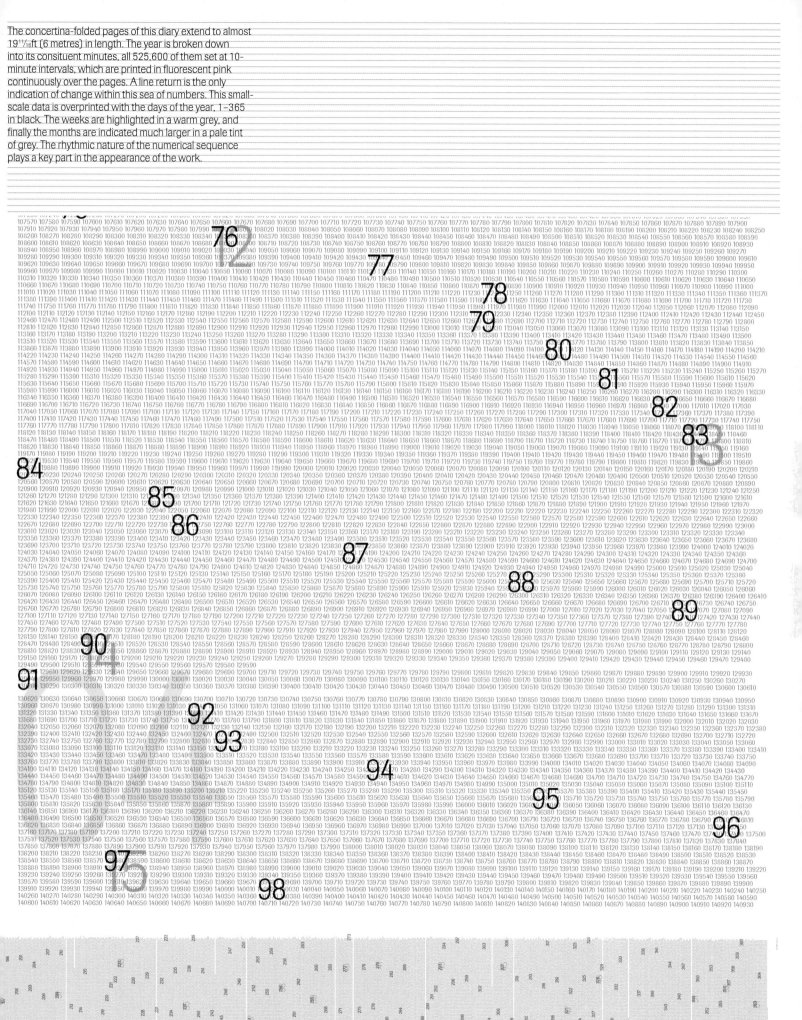

Design   Accept & Proceed
Project   Light and Dark 2007

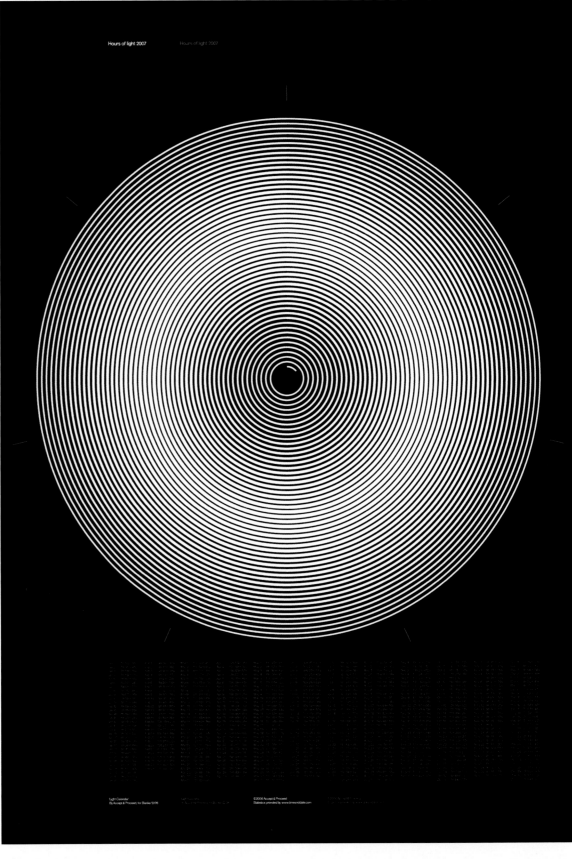

This set of two limited-edition, silkscreen-printed A1 (23⅖ x 33¹⁄₁₀in) posters charts the number of hours of daylight and darkness in the United Kingdom in 2007. The black background poster charts the number of hours of daylight, while the white poster charts the periods of darkness. Each poster is over-printed with a glow in the dark luminous ink, allowing the posters to work in both light and dark conditions.

The daylight poster illustrates the year as a series of concentric circles, with each circle representing one week, and the seven markers around the circumference indicating each day of the week.

The hours of darkness poster treats the information as a series of horizontal lines. Again, each line represents a one-week period, which is divided into the seven days of the week. Both posters also feature the same information at the bottom of the poster, indicating the number of hours of light and dark for each day of the week.

Hours of dark 2007

'Light Calendar'
By Accept & Proceed, for Blanka 12/06

©2006 Accept & Proceed
Statistics provided by www.timeanddate.com

Hours of dark 2007

Design   Accept & Proceed
Project   Light and Dark 2008

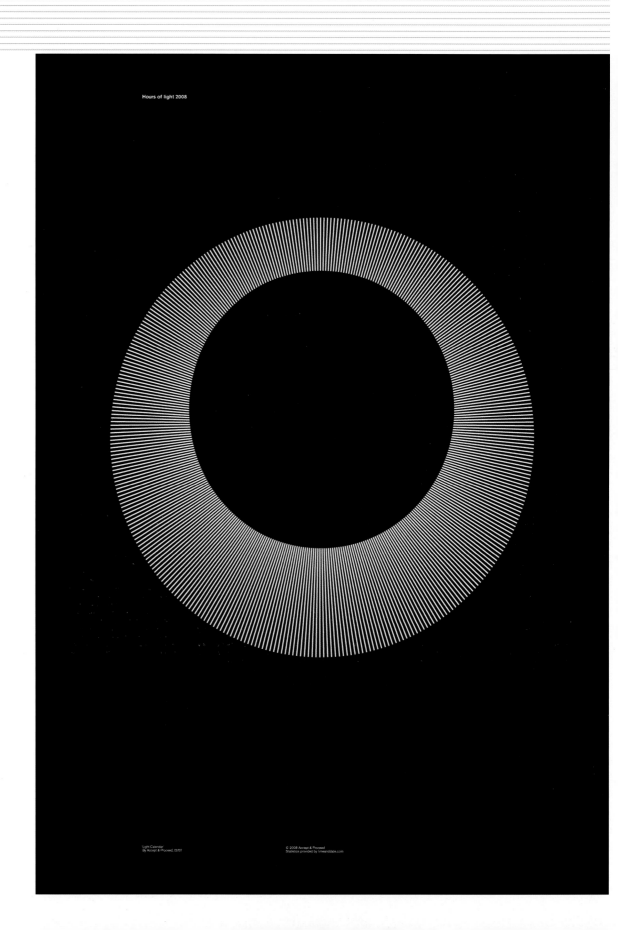

This set of two limited-edition, silkscreen-printed A1 (23⅜ x 33⅛in) posters charts the number of hours of daylight and darkness in the United Kingdom for 2008. The black background poster charts the number of hours of daylight, while the white poster charts the periods of darkness. Each poster is over-printed with a glow in the dark luminous ink, allowing the posters to work in light and dark conditions.

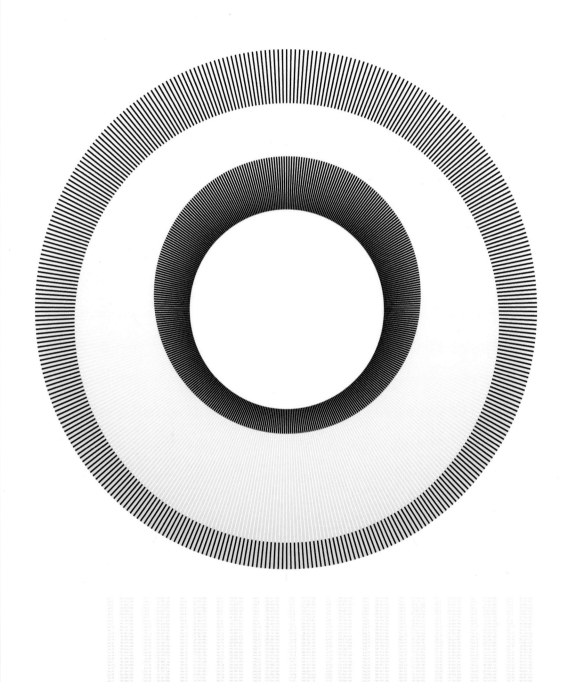

Hours of dark 2008

'Light Calendar'
By Accept & Proceed, 12/07

© 2008 Accept & Proceed
Statistics provided by timeanddate.com

Design   The Attik
Project   'NoiseFour' screen saver

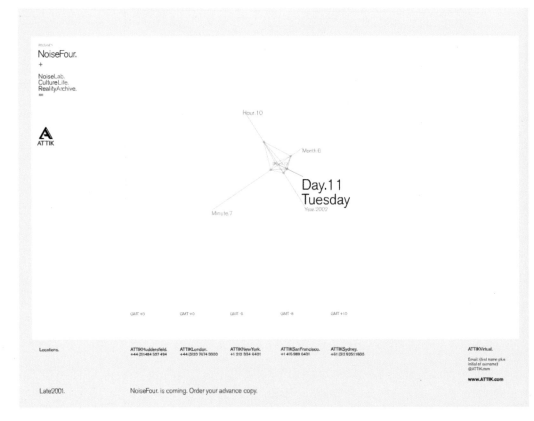

Sent out as an e-mail attachment to interested parties as a teaser for graphic design company The Attik's self-promotional book, 'NoiseFour', this screensaver, once loaded onto a computer, works as a three-dimensional clock showing seconds, minutes, hours, months, year and day of the week. The user can 'spin' the co-ordinates around by interacting with the clock using the mouse, causing the different time units to come to the fore. The appearance of the clock can also be manipulated further by dragging the time units forward which increases the size of the type on screen. This allows the user to have great control over which units of time they wish to see most prominently displayed.

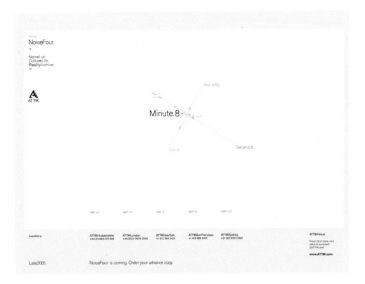

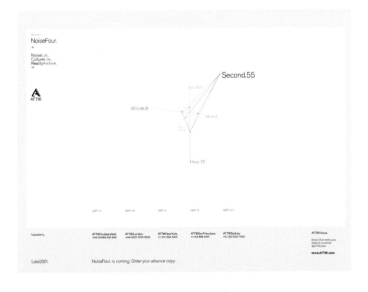

Design   Spin
Project   'Twenty-four Hours'

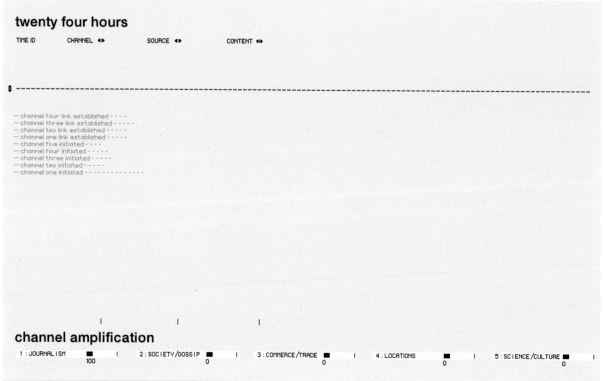

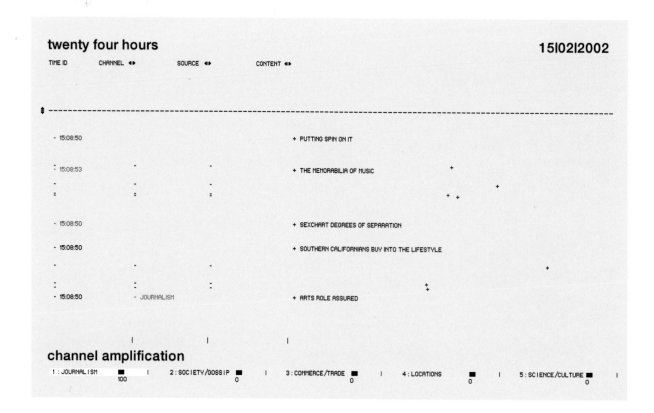

'Twenty-four Hours' is a self-initiated on-line project by
Spin, a London based multi-disciplinary design company.
The interface scans news information from various
international sources and uploads the data onto the web
site. The data, which first appears as a timecode, title
and source, can be 'amplified' to show the full news story.
Different filters can be used to channel the source material
to personalise the information. The project has been built
as a small homage to the millions of bits that make up
the avalanche of information available on the web 24
hours a day.

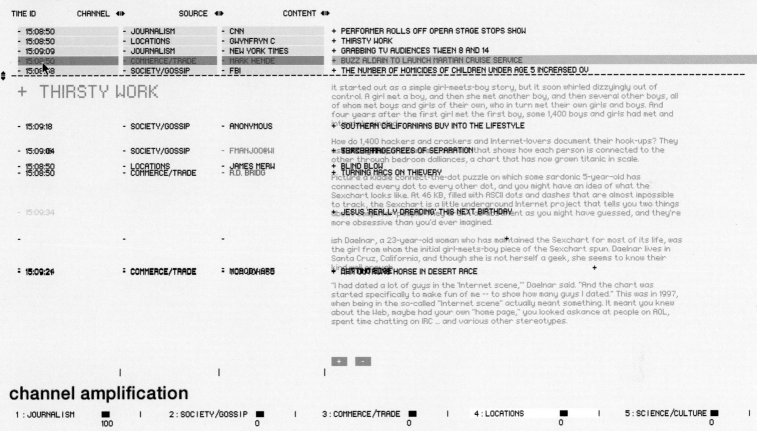

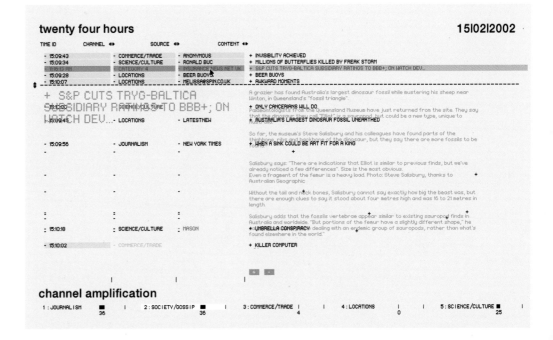

Design	Foundation 33
Project	Numerical Time Based Sound Composition
Composer	Daniel Eatock
Musician	Timothy Evans

This is a personal project by Foundation 33, exploring the point at which an audio experiment/composition becomes visual, or the point at which a visual composition becomes audible. The project moves into the realms of the concrete, where the visual is inseparable from the audio, one is not complete without the other. The piece is sent as an A3 (11⁷⁄₁₀ x 16½in) sheet of paper with the tonal bands printed on it, together with the audio CD mounted on a sheet of pulp board.

The explanatory text reads as follows:
'A digital time display counts to one hour using four units: seconds, tens of seconds, minutes, tens of minutes. A numerical sound composition has been constructed using the ten sequential digits: 0, 1, 2, 3, 4, 5, 6, 7, 8, 9. Each digit has been assigned a tone. The tones are mathematically selected from a range of 20Hz to 20,000Hz – the two extremes audible to the human ear. The tones are logarithmically divided between the ten digits providing tonal increments that produce a musical scale. Every second a different combination of four tones is defined by the time counter.'

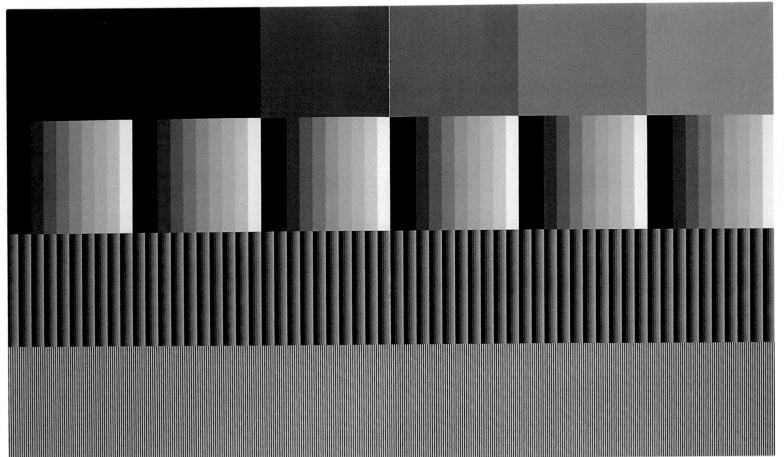

Numerical Time Based Sound Composition

Composer: Daniel Eatock / Musician: Timothy Evans

A digital time display counts to one hour using four units: seconds; tens of seconds; minutes; tens of minutes.

A numerical sound composition has been constructed using the ten sequential digits: 0, 1, 2, 3, 4, 5, 6, 7, 8, 9.

Each digit has been assigned a tone. The tones are mathematically selected from the range of 20Hz to 20,000Hz; the two extremes audible to the human ear.

The tones are logarithmically divided between the ten digits providing tonal increments that produce a musical scale.

Every second a different combination of four tones is defined by the time counter.

Above is a diagram that represents the hour long composition.

Foundation 33
33 Temple Street
London
E2 6QQ

020 7739 9903
info@foundation33.com

Design   Cartlidge Levene
Project   Canal Building brochure

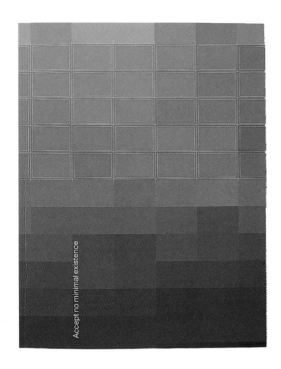

Accept no minimal existence

A clever brochure designed to promote a development of apartments in Islington, London, includes photographs of the raw, unmodernised interior shell of the building, as the brochure was produced prior to the start of the redevelopment. A large section of the lavish brochure is dedicated to a map of the surrounding area, but unusually, the map is purely photographic, and no diagrams of streets and roads are included. The map is based on the walking times to various local amenities, but these routes are illustrated with more abstract images of tree bark, water and concrete. This mapping method is useful to people not familiar with the area, as it shows with a flick of the pages the texture of area the development is set within.

Towards the back of the brochure are two further maps, one a conventional line drawing of the area, and the other an aerial photograph showing a larger area of London. This image is overlaid with a grid system on a scale which equates to a three-minute walk for each square on the grid. A series of numbers is also printed on the image which relates to the page number of the photographic mapping system, allowing the two views to be cross-referenced.

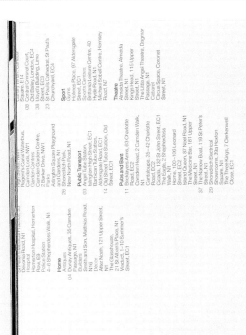

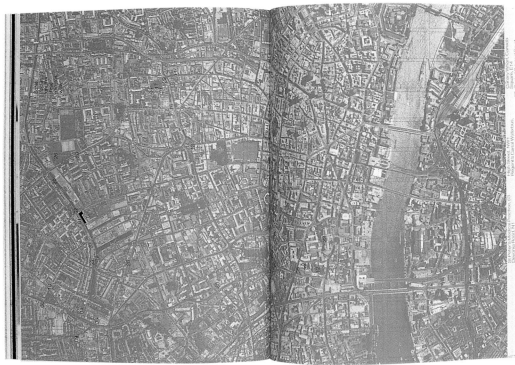

Design   Sagmeister Inc.
Project   'Made You Look' timeline

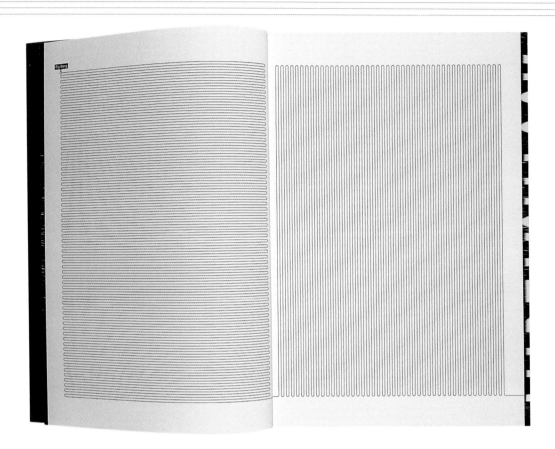

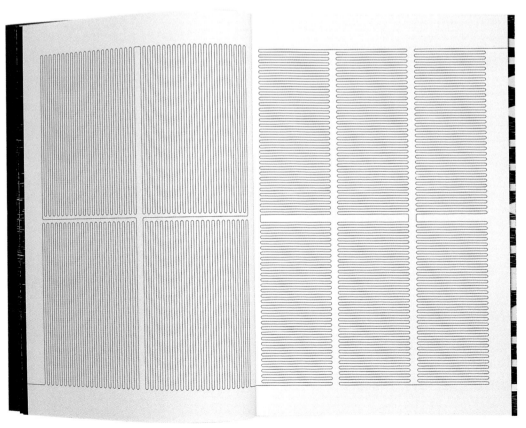

'Made You Look' is a collection of the work of New York-based graphic designer Stefan Sagmeister. At the beginning of the book is a timeline, which extends over the course of eight pages. The timeline is just that, a line that weaves its way back and forth across and up and down the page in a clean and pure fashion. At the top of the first page a small circle is annotated with the words 'Big Bang'. Nothing further happens until the sixth page, where another annotated circle is flagged 'Earth sees light of day'. The final two pages see a quickening of pace, towards the bottom of the pages 'Green blue algae appear,

Jellyfish evolve, Plants appear, Amphibians come alive, Marine reptiles appear, Dinosaurs start to flourish, Birds emerge', and so on, until just before the end of the line, 'Neanderthals appear' and finally 'The entire history of graphic design'.

A footnote reads as follows: 'The little circle representing the entire history of graphic design is of course shown much too large here: In real life and scale it is about 1/100 000 of an inch, which is a very, very small circle. Now, my whole working life: Too bitsy to think about. That Aerosmith job that went on forever? Oh boy.'

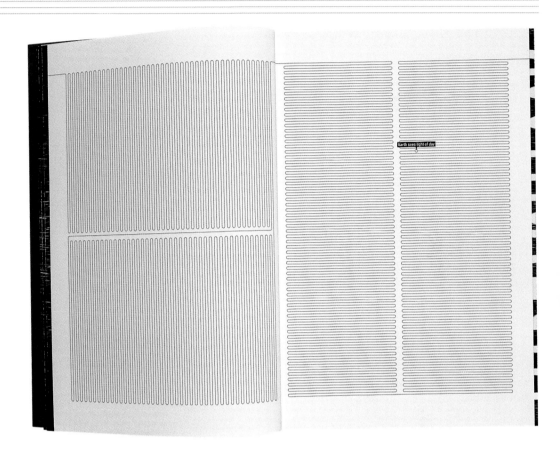

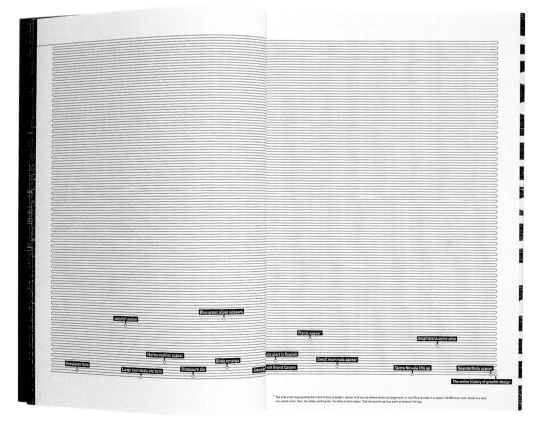

Design   Mark Diaper
Artist   Tony Oursler
Project   'The Influence Machine'

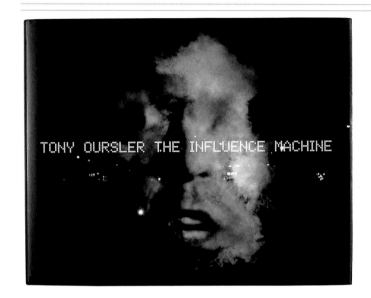

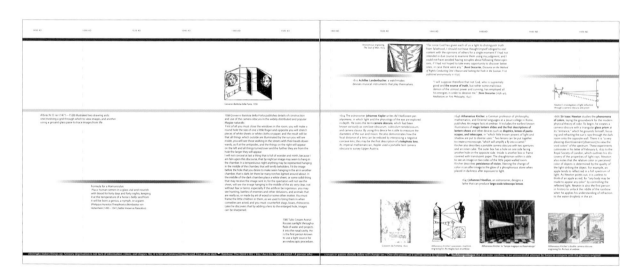

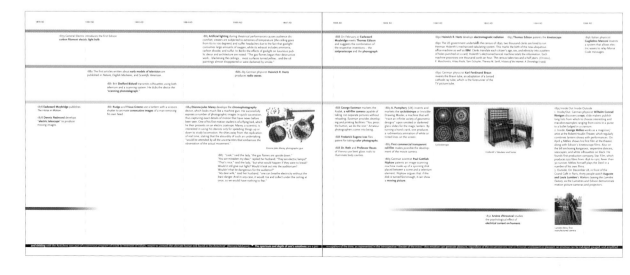

'Timestream: I hate the dark. I love the light' is a timeline developed by the artist Tony Oursler and designed by Mark Diaper for the Artangel/Public Art Fund book, 'The Influence Machine'. The timeline, which extends over 26 pages of the book, is intended to chart the history of religion/mythology/philosophy, optics/still and moving images, computers/the Internet, physics/mechanics/electronics, telecommunications, quackery/the occult/spiritualism. A specific colour is attributed to each of these broad categories and is plotted horizontally over the pages starting in the 5th–2nd centuries BC with the Egyptian god Seth and ending with the Endoscope pill camera in 2000 AD.

The colour bars for each strand of information fade in and out and swerve up and down to make space for the various entries. Interestingly the red bar used to represent religion/mythology/philosophy fades out around 1705 AD as the orange of physics/mechanics/electronics becomes prominent.

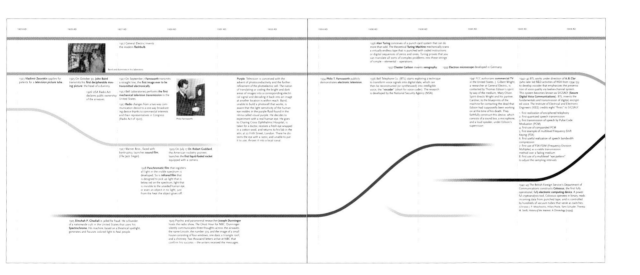

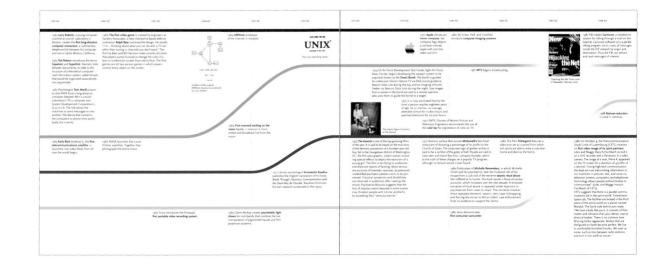

Design   Nina Naegal and A. Kanna
Project   Time/Emotions

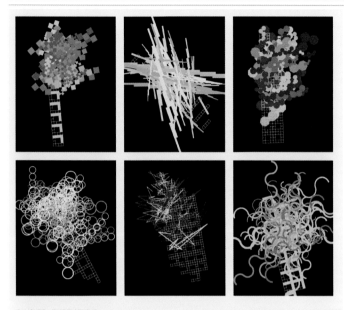

24 HOURS – TIME/EMOTIONS (in collaboration with A. Kanna)
'Time /Emotions' is a new system to read the time. It's visualised by two combined patterns. The first pattern symbolises the actual time and there fore it's created by a rule which uses the figures of that time as a guide. The second pattern which shows the emotions is made out of many different shapes which were put down by a rule, determining the shape, size, colour, rotation of the shape and placement of the shapes on the grid. As the grid to put down the second pattern we used the first pattern as the emotions hinge on that moment of time.The final pattern visualises the new system 'Time/Emotions'.

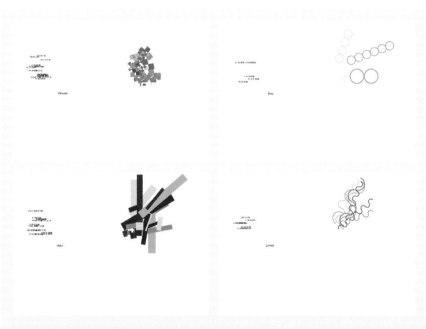

24 HOURS (24 books in slip case)
The system'Time/Emotions' runs through 24 hours. Every hour has been analysed according
to our emotions and has then been put through the two rules to visualise the system of reading the time.
shown above> spreads of magazine accompanying exhibition

'Time/Emotions' was developed by Nina Naegal and A. Kanna as a new method for reading time. The image is generated by the overlaying of two different patterns; the first is a grid system formed by a time sequence, this gives a uniform base grid. The emotional pattern is then placed over the time grid. The emotional patterns are made out of many different shapes which are placed by a rule, determining the contours, size, colour and rotation of the shape as well as the position of the shapes on the time grid.

Shown here are pages from a 24-part book which shows the various stages of emotion. Also shown is an A1 (23⅖ x 33¹⁄₁₀in) poster related to the project.

Artist   Jem Finer
Project   Long Player

Commissioned by Artangel, Longplayer was developed by Jem Finer and managed by Candida Blaker with a think-tank comprising artist and musician Brian Eno, British Council Director of Music John Kieffer, landscape architect Georgina Livingston, Artangel co-director Michael Morris, digital sound artist Joel Ryan, architect and writer Paul Shepheard and writer and composer David Toop. Longplayer was conceived as a 1000-year musical composition, which began playing on 1st of January 2000 and will play continuously and without repetition until 31st of December 2999.

Longplayer can be heard at listening posts in the United Kingdom, with plans to establish other listening posts at diverse sites around the world. The first site was established in a disused lighthouse at Trinity Buoy Wharf in London Docklands. Longplayer is also planned to stream in real time on the Internet.

The music is generated by a computer playing six loops taken from a pre-recorded 20-minute, 20-second composition, each of which is of a different pitch and advances at a different speed. The constant shifting of these layers creates ever-changing textures and harmonies. The instrumentation in the source music is primarily Tibetan singing bowls of various sizes.

Technology is embraced as a means to share an experience not only of music but also of a dream of time. There is no wish to send an ideological monument out into the future landscape, only the ambition to engender connections through time and space. Though it starts its life as a computer program, Longplayer works in such a way that its production is not restricted to just one form of technology. The resilience of Longplayer will be evidenced by its ability to adapt rather than to endure in its original form.

Design   Studio Myerscough
Project   Forest of Infinity

To celebrate the 25th anniversary of the specialist furniture
supplier Coexistence, graphic design consultancy Studio
Myerscough designed both a commemorative book
and an exhibition held at the RIBA architecture gallery
in London.
                    The exhibition was set out as a three-
dimensional timeline showing classic pieces of furniture
design which have been produced over the last 25 years.
Each item was positioned under a white lozenge-shaped
lampshade with the year printed on which was suspended
from the ceiling. The captions explaining each exhibit were
printed next to the item on the floor.

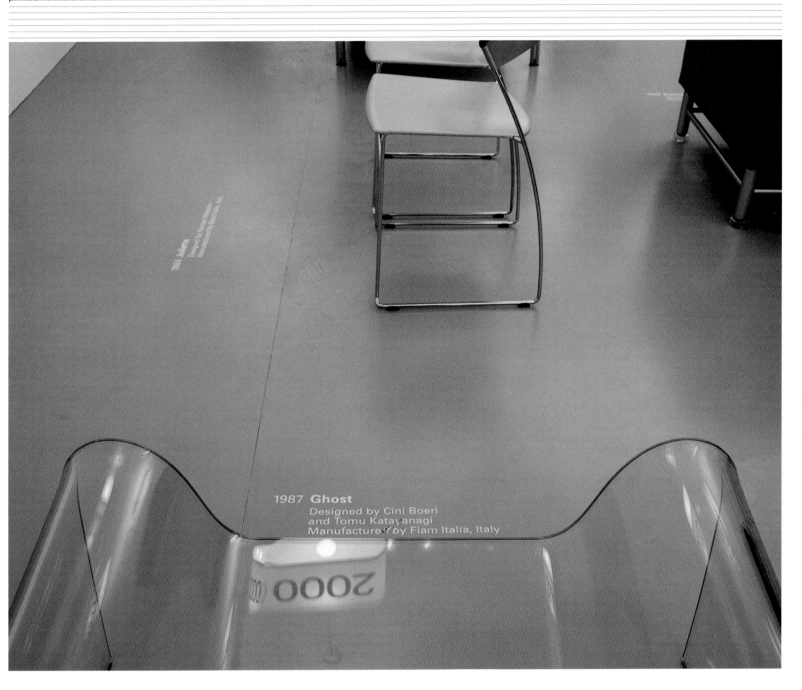

1987 **Ghost**
Designed by Cini Boeri
and Tomu Katayanagi
Manufactured by Fiam Italia, Italy

Design   Studio Myerscough
Project   Web Wizards

60 70 80 90 00

	1963	1964	1968	1969	1971	1972	1973	1974	1975	1976	1977	1978	1979	1980	1981	1982	1983	1984	1985	1986	1987	1988	1989	1990	1991	1992	1993	1994	1995	1996	1997	1998	1999	2000	2001	2002	
Technological developments																																					Technological developments
Hardware																																					Hardware
Software																																					Software
Arcade games																																					Arcade games
Home consoles																																					Home consoles
Digital Art and Design																																					Digital Art and Design

'Webwizards' was an exhibition held at the Design Museum in London, presenting some of the most innovative contemporary on-line art and design work. The exhibition, designed by Studio Myerscough, included a large scale timeline charting the history of computers and the Internet from the 1960s to the present day, which was printed along an entire wall.

Exhibits were connected with each other via lines printed across floors and walls, which made the entire event interrelated, with objects treated like coordinates within a virtual computer world.

Acknowledgments

I would like to extend my deep thanks to all those who have helped
in creating this book, whether by kindly submitting work or for help
and advice.

A special thank you should be extended to William Owen for his
insight; Ben Tappenden for his great enthusiasm; Sanne, Tristan,
Minnie and Monty for their constant support and understanding;
Chris Foges, Laura Owen and all at RotoVision for their faith
and patience.

rf-t